RADICAL SPIRITUALITY

D1310962

RADICAL SPIRITUALITY

Metaphysical Awareness For A New Century

DICK SUTPHEN

Other Metaphysical Books by Dick Sutphen

(Simon & Schuster Pocket Books)

You Were Born Again To Be Together
Past Lives, Future Loves
Unseen Influences
Predestined Love
Finding Your Answers Within
Earthly Purpose
The Oracle Within

(Valley of the Sun Publishing)

Master of Life Manual
Enlightenment Transcripts
Lighting The Light Within
Past-Life Therapy In Action
Sedona
Heart Magic
The Spiritual Path Guidebook
Reinventing Yourself

Also From Valley of the Sun

Over 300 audio/video self-help and self-exploration tape titles, and a line of inner-harmony music. *Master of Life Winners* is a quarterly magazine mailed free to 200,000 book/tape buyers. Write for a copy.

© 1995 by Dick Sutphen, Box 38, Malibu, CA 90265. All rights reserved. "Bushido" and "Master of Life" are registered trademarks of The Sutphen Corporation, Box 38, Malibu, CA 90265. No part of this book may be reproduced in any form without written permission from the publisher, except for brief passages included in a review in a newspaper or magazine. Cover Photos: © Deb Fritz Wycislak—*Flames*; © Ed Wanner—*Bird*.

Printed in the United States of America.
First Edition: May 1995
Valley of the Sun Publishing, Box 38, Malibu, CA 90265

ISBN Number 0-87554-583-1
Library of Congress Card Number 94-90778

To Tara,
Hunter & Cheyenne

CONTENTS

CHAPTER 1

LIFE IS SPIRITUALITY

*"Among the most remarkable features characterizing
Zen we find these: spirituality, directness of
expression, disregard of form or conventionalism,
and frequently an almost wanton delight in going
astray from respectability."*
—*D.T. Suzuki*

In the early 70s, my martial-arts sensei introduced me to Zen ... which led to an exploration of reincarnation ... which led to studying the occult ... which led to establishing a hypnosis research center ... which led to writing books. The publication of *You Were Born Again To Be Together* (Pocket Books 1976) created a demand for more books, seminars and tapes ... and I embarked on a full-time metaphysical career.

Looking back, I'm thankful it all started with Zen—a process of seeking to find in self, opposed to ceremony or doctrine, a path to wisdom. Zen is neither a religion nor a philosophy, but a way of liberation—a game of discovering who you are beneath the social masks. The Zen trainee is encouraged to leap into the unknown and find the true self within. The true self is found when the fearful self is renounced.

Zen exists today because it was embraced by the Samurai who valued a mentally independent and spiritually powerful way of being—men and women known for their strength of character, tranquility and detachment. In their acceptance of reincarnation, they rose above the fear of death. In studying reincarnation, I found that karma explained the injustice and inequality in the world. No religion or philosophy could offer any other acceptable explanation. My spiritual cup began to fill.

While Samurai men are remembered for their bravery and swordsmanship, they also expressed their feminine side with art and poetry. All abilities were developed to transcend the feeling that "I am doing it" by ceasing to dwell upon winning or losing. You simply do your best, responding to an inner direction that carries you effortlessly through the experience. This thinking, this heritage, this awareness became my model—grounded metaphysics combined with street-wise Zen.

With this background, I find it difficult to relate to such concepts as the harmonic convergence, earth-change prophecy, conspiracies, UFOs, the inner-child, and lovey-dovey wonderment. Not that there isn't some reality hidden among the fairy dust, but few are served by such involvement. All too often, these aspects of the spiritual search reflect wishful or deluded thinking and keep seekers from focusing upon the real quest. The purpose of this book is to simplify the spiritual quest and,in so doing, separate the grain from the chaff.

Some of the writing in *Radical Spirituality* is new. Some is taken from seminar talks. Articles and research reports were originally published in *Master of Life WINNERS* and *Reincarnation Report* magazines. Previously published material has been edited to avoid duplicating a point covered elsewhere in the book (a few points are purposely repeated). The questions and answers are from my "Controversial Questions" column in *Master of Life Winners* magazine (1986-1995). The identification of those asking the questions has been removed for this volume.

The dialogues between myself and seminar participants have been reconstructed from audio-tape recordings made in Bushido, Satori, and Master of Life Seminars. Some have been edited to more quickly make a point. Outside the context of a seminar or counseling session, these encounters can appear cold and unfeeling. In reality, I have one goal in mind—to create the space for the individual to help him/herself, by discovering inner truths. In the seminars, I use attitudes and words as a stick to jab participants who aren't "getting it." One participant might react best to shock, another to gentle support, another to teasing. My goal is to guide the individual to become aware of self-defeating attitudes and behavior, and to jolt them out of intellectual ruts, passé notions, and convictions restricting their life. To be effective, I must be willing to incur their dislike.

Some of the content in the following chapters may have you asking, "Why is this included in a book about spirituality?" My response is that everything you think, say and do creates karma, including the motive, intent and desire behind everything you think, say and do. That being the case, every aspect of life relates to spirituality. Or ... *life is spirituality!*

CHAPTER 2

AN INTRODUCTION TO A MASTER OF LIFE VIEWPOINT IN 19 DIALOGUES

1.

"I came into this workshop angry with you about things you've written, and now I'm even more upset," said Angelia, a woman in her early forties with short-cropped brown hair. She hid excess weight beneath a loose-fitting dress and shawl.

Two hundred people were gathered in the hotel ballroom. Angelia spoke into a microphone, her voice reverberating through the room.

"Do you want to tell us why you're angry, Angelia?" I said.

"Some of the things you say about our spiritual beliefs," she said, scowling.

"You'd rather I deny what is and pander to New Age correctness?"

"Oh, come on."

"You should thank me for projecting your shadow-side."

"What's that mean?"

"I'm reflecting what's unresolved within you—a mirror for fearful emotions you need to integrate. It's a great opportunity."

"This is ridiculous. You're unaccepting of things we all believe," she said, crossing her arms while managing to hold the microphone to her lips.

"Beliefs such as think only positive thoughts, attain enlightenment, lead a selfless life, become a projection of love, meditate, meditate, meditate? Things like that?"

"For starters."

"Doesn't work, Angelia. It denies reality and ignores an unconscious balance that must be manifested. It's an attitude that keeps life from fully expressing itself."

"I fully express my life. And I think positive thoughts ninety-eight percent of the time."

"Like right now?"

She laughed. "You're part of the two percent."

"So when angry, jealous, greedy, judgmental, or prejudicial thoughts come into your mind, you just push them aside and refuse to acknowledge them?"

"That's right," she said.

"You drive them down into your unconscious, where they remain, festering?"

"I see it as rising above them."

"You think they're gone?"

She shrugged.

"They're not gone, Angelia. They've been repressed ... avoided, and now they're festering, waiting for an opportunity to be expressed."

"What do you mean, expressed?"

"Maybe you'll get an ulcer, or yell at someone who doesn't deserve it, or you might repress for years until your shadow side manifests as arthritis, or cancer, or ..."

Angelia interrupted, "But you talk about how the mind functions like a computer—positive begets positive and negative begets negative."

"Only real positive can beget positive. When you limit the expression of life, you're repressing, which begets negative."

"Well, how do you get around it?" she said, her frustration

evident.

"If you feel anger but deny or refuse to express it, you're repressing, which is fear. But to recognize the anger and dismiss it without emotion is an expression of detached mind. True detachment can only result from expanded awareness."

I turned my attention to all the seminar participants. "When you draw boundaries and say, 'I'll never think negative thoughts,' or 'I'll always do this,' or 'I'll never do that,' you pit your willpower against your unconscious, but it never works. Your unconscious will always find a way to balance life."

2.

"How can you put down selfless service?" said Janie, a woman of about fifty with long greying hair. She wore several bold pieces of Native American jewelry.

"It doesn't exist."

"Oh really? Well, I've devoted the last five years of my life to taking care of my dying father. I would much rather have enjoyed myself, dated, taken some vacations."

"What would you think of a daughter who left her father to die with uncaring strangers, Janie?"

"Someone utterly lacking in compassion, who is also creating negative karma."

"You see yourself as being a loving, compassionate daughter?"

"Yes."

"And you would have felt terribly guilty if you had refused to care for your father?"

"He doesn't have anyone else."

"And you certainly don't want to create negative karma?"

She shook her head.

"So you did it for yourself, Janie. Just like everyone else on the planet, you lived up to your self-image of being a good daughter, and you avoided painful guilt. Your father was served, but you did it for yourself."

No response.

"You can stop fooling yourself about why you do what you do."

No response.

"You can stop waiting for a gold star."

3.

"Most of you are seeking enlightenment, and you think you're going to find it by looking under a white light or through some cosmic foo-foo spiritual discipline," I said, noticing a few scowls. Many of the seminar participants began crossing their arms, signaling closed communications. I pushed harder. "First of all, there is no such thing as enlightenment! You're going to have to settle for self-actualization."

"This is ridiculous," said a young man in his mid-twenties. He had raised his hand, and without waiting to be acknowledged, stood up and began speaking before the support team member arrived with a microphone. "I've been studying spirituality for six years, and I didn't come here to be told there is no such thing as enlightenment."

I walked up the aisle until close enough to read his name tag. "Sorry, Phil, but many of the things you believe are not true. You've accepted beliefs about people and philosophy and truth that have helped you to survive, but you've been conned. So has everyone else in this room."

"You don't know anything!" Phil sputtered.

"I know that the level of your success in life will depend on your ability to let go of fear and mistaken beliefs."

"Well, I know absolutely that there are many enlightened souls upon the earth. Obviously, you aren't one of them," Phil said.

"No, I'm not, but I'd like you to show me one. Are you speaking of the big names in the spiritual field? The famous Oriental or Middle Eastern gurus, or the bestselling metaphysical authors, or the channelers, or the human-potential leaders?"

"Sure."

"I don't think so, Phil. Many of these people are personal friends, who are doing wonderful work, and many are certainly self-actualized, but not enlightened. At least a dozen other leaders in the New Age/human-potential field have been involved in major public scandals in the last few years. I'm afraid that those who claim to be enlightened, aren't."

"Maybe we don't define enlightened the same way," Phil said.

"Well, wouldn't an enlightened soul have attained freedom *from* the self? Freedom from domination by their addictions, obsessions, dependencies, and passions? Wouldn't he have resolved or integrated his fear-based emotions?"

Phil nodded.

"Enlightenment isn't some 'thing' to attain, Phil. Enlightenment is freedom from the self, which is an **absence** of fears, or in the least, the ability to experience fear without responding to fear."

"Semantic games?" Phil said, scowling.

"I'm trying to make a point. There is no such thing as enlightenment. It's a non-thing, an absence," I said.

"There are a lot of people who have attained freedom from the self," Phil said firmly.

"Really? People who never get upset by circumstances or the actions of others? They never judge others? They totally accept what is? They never take anything personally? They never smile when they don't feel like smiling? They ..."

"What do you mean, smile when they don't feel like smiling?" Phil interrupted.

"If you smile when you don't feel like smiling, you're not being direct and honest in your communications. You're wearing a mask and repressing who you really are. That's just a little bitty fear, but fear nonetheless. You fear that others won't like you if you don't smile. Or you'll feel uncomfortable if you don't make them feel more comfortable, or ..."

"Got it!" Phil said, sitting down.

4.

Returning my attention to all the seminar participants, I said, "For years I've been telling people that from a karmic perspective, fear-based emotions are nothing more than delusions programmed by current-life and past-life experiences. As you become self-actualized, you become aware of what is, and let go of the fears. Your earthly purpose, then, can be simplified down to just four words: *Cast away your delusions*, or if you prefer, *Learn to let go.* Take your choice. It amounts to *detachment.*

"To be more accurate, when talking about integrating fears, I should say, 'Your earthly purpose is to integrate the *neurotic* fears that keep you earthbound.' Examples of neurotic fears are prejudice, aggressiveness, anger, selfishness, jealousy, hate, repression, envy, greed, possessiveness, guilt ... and fear of intimacy, loss, abandonment, failure, loneliness, success, and power ... just to name a few.

"To avoid a bear in the woods, to stay out of the wrong part of town at night, or to refrain from addictive drugs are fears based upon real dangers.

"By contrast, neurotic fears are based on issues you have failed to integrate on a soul level, which keep you from experiencing 'wholeness.' As an example, let's say you're prejudiced toward East Indians. They somehow represent a subjective threat. When an East Indian couple moves next door, at first you're upset and reticent about contact. But there's no way to avoid meeting as you come and go, water the lawn, pick up your mail. In time, you grow to like your new neighbors, and they become friends. The fear is integrated—replaced by a greater potential to enjoy life—and you are one step closer to wholeness.

"In this situation, it would be accurate to say, love let in what fear shut out ... or integration resulted in detachment ... or integration *is* detachment.

"It follows that your current problems are rooted in one or more fear-based emotions. The fears go back to unintegrated issues, and they are your karma—the soul lessons you've reincarnated to learn."

5.

"How is anyone ever going to integrate all their fearful emotions?" asked Jennifer, a pretty blonde woman in her thirties wearing the latest Melrose Avenue fashions.

"Well, it can't happen unless you give it importance," I said. "Integrating a fear amounts to reprogramming a negative belief with a positive belief. In other words, expanding your awareness. Change takes time. You have to work at it."

"But it's such a difficult task, why even bother?"

"Because your life will work better and better in direct relationship to your ability to integrate your fears. Even a little effort at understanding will result in improvements."

"I'm sure you'd claim fighting with my husband is based on fear," she said.

"Sure. You want approval or control or you wouldn't fight. Both actions are manifestations of the fear of not getting what you want."

"I don't understand."

"You want your husband to approve of your actions or reactions, or you want to control his actions or reactions. He wants the same thing."

"I want him to stop criticizing me."

"You want to control his actions."

"Well, I guess so, if that's what it takes to get him to stop."

"You make my point, Jennifer. But let's take this a little further and explore it from a self-actualized viewpoint. Is your husband normally a critical person?"

"Yes, he's always been critical of everything and everybody."

"Always? Then do you think he is going to change?"

"Not really."

"You married him, knowing that he was a critical person?"

"Yes, but ..."

"Do you want out of the marriage?"

"No, absolutely not. I love him."

"Okay, you can't change another person. He has to want to change and be willing to work at it. That doesn't sound too likely, although I would suggest that you calmly express your needs in this area. But for the moment, if you don't think he'll change, and you're upset by the criticism, it sounds to me like it's up to you to change how you respond to your husband."

"Hmmm," she murmured.

"What if your husband were married to a different woman ... a woman named Sally who looked different, but did the same basic things you do. Would he be critical of her?"

"I know he would."

"Then the problem is taking the criticism personally. Most problems in life are not resolved by an actual change but by a change in viewpoint. If you could develop 'detached mind,' you'd stop taking things personally. You'd know someone else's reaction to you, good or bad, is based upon their past programming. It has nothing to do with you. The way they relate to you is the way they would relate to anyone in your position. In this case, your husband is a man who would criticize any wife."

"So, I have to change my thinking?"

"Reality exists as a manifestation of your viewpoint. If you let your husband's criticism flow through you without affecting you, you integrate the fear. If you can do that, you'll no longer have a problem, although nothing will have changed but your viewpoint."

6.

"Is boredom a fear-based emotion?" asked Terry, a middle-aged man clad in a herringbone sport coat with leather elbow patches.

"Any negative emotion is based on fear," I said. "Boredom is a loud message. It's saying, 'I'm living wrong!'"

"What do you mean?" Terry asked.

"The human mind cannot tolerate boredom for long. The brain/mind professionals have documented that if you don't make your life interesting and meaningful, your mind will do it for you. It will generate conflicts, or illness, or an accident. Anything to make life more interesting!"

"But I can't help it that I'm bored," he said.

"Terry, you're bored because there's no challenge in your life. Whose responsibility is that, if not yours? It's time to live a little more dangerously and start risking. When you do, your boredom will disappear."

7.

"Freedom from yourself will evolve out of a new way of thinking ... a self-actualized, Master of Life way of thinking. Self-examination is the first step. Examine your beliefs, your reactions, your concerns. You can't change what you don't recognize."

"I'm a perfectionist. Is that a fear?" asked a stern-looking young woman.

"Most perfectionists are neurotics. That's pretty fearful. Are you neurotic, Betty?"

"I don't think so," she said.

"What is your reaction when you don't do a job perfectly?"

"Ah, well, I guess I feel guilty. Sure, I feel guilty, real guilty."

"Have you answered your own question?"

She was silent for a moment, then said, "Okay, but what do I do about it?"

"I suggest that you begin by finding the cause of your neurosis. Everything we feel relates to a cause, which is based on a past event or series of events that have programmed us to be the way we are. But no matter what the past cause, change will come through self-actualized awareness in the present."

At this point in the seminar, I directed a group Back-to-the-Cause Regression, telling the hypnotized participants, "You will go back to the cause of the situation you've decided to investigate. The cause will be found earlier in your present life or in one of your many past lives."

After the session Betty said, "My mother died when I was only five in this life, so I don't know for sure if this is true. But in hypnosis, I relived a situation in which she spanked me and spanked me and spanked me. I was probably about three years old, and had gotten into her sewing kit and thrown the pieces all over the room. Mother became hysterical and told me to put everything back in the case, exactly as it was. If I didn't do it perfectly, she would spank me until I did. I think I spent the entire afternoon futilely trying to get it perfect. She'd leave the room, come back a few minutes later to check the box, spank me and repeat the process. I was so scared I shook."

"Do you get that you no longer need to put the sewing kit back together, Betty?" I said, laughing.

8.

"Pessimism must also be fear," said Walter, a fortyish, balding man, dressed very conservatively.

I nodded in response.

"I wasn't always a pessimist. In my youth, I was pretty optimistic, but how can anyone go through the experiences of life without seeing how it works? It's f—ked! I'm just a realist, acknowledging life for what it is."

"A pessimist is filled with anger because life hasn't been fair, or so he thinks. Because life doesn't work the way he wants it to work, he blames life for his problems. Right, Walter?"

No response.

"RIGHT, WALTER?"

"Right," he mumbled.

"Playing the part of a victim and blaming others for your circumstances is a useless expression of self-pity. Would you like us to pity you, Walter?"

"Don't bother."

"Well, what about the programming power of pessimism? Now that's heavy. Your mind is a bio-computer that creates your reality based on your thoughts and emotions. The more pessimistic you are, the more miserable your life becomes. It's an automatic downward spiral. Are you having a wonderful life, Walter?"

"No, and this seminar is just as stupid as I expected it would be," he replied, stalking out of the room.

9.

"Let's not get stuck on the obvious fears," I said. "Anyone with an addiction, dependency, or obsession is not free. And anyone dominated by their passions is not free."

"I can't see that following your passions is a bad thing," said John, an overweight young man in his late twenties, wearing a bulky sweater.

"Being passionate isn't bad, John. But if your passions take control, causing you to ignore reason, you're being dominated by your passions. You might have such a passion for food that you indulge to the point of obesity. I don't think you want that. When you're driven to do something that isn't serving you, you're not free."

"What about sexual passions?" he asked.

"If your sexual passions cause you to do things that result in loss of self-esteem or endanger your primary relationship or your life, the answer is pretty obvious, isn't it?"

10.

"I really dislike someone I work with. In fact, I hate him. But in this case, it isn't fear, it's wisdom. Ayn Rand says that we must never fail to pronounce moral judgment," said Linda, a thin woman, mid-thirties, dressed in a sport coat and jeans.

"Although I often agree with Ayn Rand, we're at odds on judgment. But if you're a fan of hers, you also know she says that hatred is generated by profound self-doubt, self-condemnation and fear. Hate generates programming that will draw what you hate back to you. What you resist, you attract, because you need to learn from it. You'll continue to draw the hated person or someone with the same tendencies into your life until you can release this fear. Examine hate in the light of the Universal Law of Attraction: Where your attention goes, your energy flows. You attract the qualities you possess. If you want peace and harmony in your life, you must become peaceful and harmonious."

11.

"I've been studying these things for 30 years, Richard," said an elderly lady who remained seated while speaking into the microphone. "I've certainly changed my life for the better because of my expanded awareness, but I have a problem with the fear of insecurity. I don't think any of us are ever going to eliminate insecurity. Life is insecure. Love is insecure. We're always moving from the known to the unknown."

"Joanne, if you were to attain total security in a particular area, you would soon become bored with that aspect of your life. There would be no challenge and it would become dull and mundane. Maybe it's time to transform the way you experience insecurity, because it's the unknown and unknowable that makes life exciting. Insecurity generates the rush, the titillation, the thrill of aliveness. Instead of fearing insecurity, embrace it, thank it."

12.

"How can you get past anger?" asked Jason, a male in his late twenties who had already disclosed to the seminar participants that he was gay and his ex-lover had tested positive for AIDS. "I don't mean intellectually, but emotionally how do you let go of anger?" His voice was pained.

"I think it has to start with logical understanding, Jason. Just knowing that anger quickly turns into destructiveness is a pretty good place to begin. Each time you get angry, you are mentally programming negativity, which is self-destructive."

We discussed other aspects of anger, and my words were registering, but Jason only nodded passively. "That's logical, but it doesn't help much."

"The real problem with anger is in repressing it," I continued. "That's an avoidance tactic, which will drive it deeper into your subconscious, where the resentment spreads like a cancer. First, you need to understand the anger intellectually; next, you need to experience it. Until you totally experience something, you cannot integrate it."

"How do I totally experience my anger?" Jason asked.

"By expressing it cleanly to the proper person."

"What do you mean by 'cleanly'?"

"Without blame. Without making the other person wrong. You simply express your feelings and unmet needs. Emotional intensity is desirable, but your tone of voice must not be accusing or it won't be a clean expression of anger."

"What if the other person is wrong?" he asked.

"The human-potential response is that you and you alone are responsible for what you experience. You're choosing the experience of making the other person wrong. The metaphysical response is that blame is incompatible with karma. You only experience what you karmically need to experience, so the other person is just helping you to learn. My personal response is that blame is always self-pity and doesn't do anything but make matters worse."

"What if I can't express my anger in person? I don't even know where he is—he left town." Jason's voice started to break, and tears formed in the corners of his eyes.

"It isn't absolutely necessary to express anger to anyone else to affect it. You could go off by yourself, or you could find some friends who are willing to listen. Rant and rave! Make it worse! Be a poor baby! Tell everybody what you think! Don't stop until you're so exhausted, you feel a release. It might take a few minutes or a few hours of catharsis, but when you're done, you will have transcended the emotions. And we could start right here, right now, Jason." I yelled at him, "TELL ME ABOUT YOUR ANGER! WHAT THE F—K DO YOU HAVE TO BE ANGRY ABOUT?"

After 15 minutes of crying, screaming and directly getting in touch with his anger, Jason collapsed into his chair, exhausted. Before the seminar was over, he shared his sense of release with the other participants. "The anger feels gone. I don't feel it any more. Thank you all for your love and support."

13.

"Sadly, although we have the ability to learn through love and wisdom, we usually choose to learn through pain. This is what karma is all about. If you get punched in the nose every time you walk through a yellow door, eventually (if you have any sense) you will stop walking through yellow doors. If you burn your finger every time you touch a hot stove, eventually you will avoid hot stoves. If you make yourself miserable for years (or lifetimes) when other people don't live up to your **expectations,** eventually you will learn it is your expectations—not other people—that are making you miserable. When your expectations are in conflict with what is (reality), you resist what is and get upset. Buddha summed up the cause of all suffering when he said, 'It is your resistance to what is that causes your suffering.'"

14.

"Just because I resist my boss doesn't mean that I'm losing

the game," said Judy, a conservatively dressed woman in her late thirties.

"It does if you're being passed over for promotion," I replied.

"But my boss is an idiot."

"And he's your boss. That's what is. I don't think you're going to change that unless you quit."

"But it's ridiculous. You can't imagine how bad this guy is," she said, twisting the microphone cable for emphasis.

"Judy, what is, is that he's your boss. He probably won't recommend you for a raise or a promotion. Your expectations are the problem."

"Damned right they are. I expect him not to be an asshole."

"But what is, is that he's an asshole."

"Right."

"Right."

"Well, it's time he changed," she said, frowning at me.

"Is that realistic?"

"Probably not."

"Well, we know what you've lost as a result of your resistance. What have you gained or what will you gain?"

She paused and looked up at the ceiling, then down at the floor. "Nothing, I guess."

"You get to be right about your boss being an asshole, but you lose the game. Wouldn't it be smarter to win the game?"

"But he's an asshole."

"JUDY! BE LOGICAL. GET IT."

"I get it, but I don't like it. It's not fair."

"Where did you get the idea that life is supposed to be fair?"

She folded her arms and stared at me. "If I accepted these ideas, I wouldn't have anything left to talk about." She laughed.

15.

"Are you saying you have to accept total responsibility for your feelings?" asked James, a distinguished-looking man in his late forties, wearing a white shirt, red tie and dark blue blazer.

"Yes," I said.

"Okay. I was recently divorced and my ex-wife put me through the wringer. Doesn't she share some responsibility for the negativity I experienced?"

"She didn't live up to your expectations of how a dear, departing wife should act?"

"Oh, come on," he snapped.

"You want to blame her?"

"All I'm saying is I'm not a hundred percent responsible for my feelings."

"This is a cliche, James, but I'll say it anyway. Short of physical violence, it isn't what someone says to you or does to you that affects you, it's what you add to it. It's what you think about what they say or do that affects you."

"I'm the one who made all the money. Her getting the house and newer car affected me."

"Your wife didn't do her part to create the lifestyle you shared?"

"Well ..."

"You made the money, she did what she did. The combined effort amounted to your lifestyle. Sounds to me like she deserved half."

"You sound like her lawyer." He was beginning to get upset.

"This is a community property state. Didn't you get your half?"

"Yes, but not the house and car. That affected me."

"You chose to let it affect you. What did you get?"

"Some investments and the second car."

"And you could sell the investments and buy another house?" No response.

"It's your resistance to what is that's causing your suffering, James."

"You have a way of twisting everything around."

16.

"I think resistance can be good," said June, a pretty young woman in her late twenties, dressed in a layered wool dress, a shawl and boots. "I resist fearful things and my life is a lot more comfortable because of it."

"What kind of fearful things?" I asked.

"The freeways, scary movies, dating guys I don't really know. Things like that."

"Is being comfortable and secure a high priority for you?"

"It sure is."

"I think it is with most people. They survive by hunkering down and remaining in their safe little corner of the world. Everything is familiar. No sweat. No strain. You handle your life right?"

"Don't make it sound negative," she said.

"It's just that I wonder if such a lifestyle can really manifest your full potential for joy? What about lack of challenge and boredom? If you don't make life interesting enough, your mind will generate problems to let you know you're alive—personal conflicts, illness, an accident. Life is not safe and secure. That's what is."

"And you think I'm resisting what is?" she said. "Well, maybe I am. But I don't mind being bored."

"But what about the depression?"

"How did you ..."

"It's usually the mind's first attempt to make life more interesting."

"Oh," she said, giving me a strange look. She gave the microphone back to the support team member and sat down.

17.

"You simplify spirituality and take all the spiritual out of it," said Norm. He was about thirty, dressed in a t-shirt and jeans.

"Life is spirituality, so how can I take the spiritual out of life?

If it makes you feel better to study dogmas, experience rituals, or work with a guru, then you may feel you have to *earn* your awareness, Norm. But in the end, it will all come down to integrating your fears."

"But being a truly spiritual person means more than that," he said.

"Does it? If you experience no fear, all that would be left would be love. How much more spiritual can you get?"

"Oh."

"There's another way to look at it. Master Eckart said, 'If you empty yourself, God enters into you."

"I like that," he said. "Fear results from ignorance of your God-self?"

"I like *that*," I said. "And maybe we're afraid because we're not really sure there is a God-self beneath all our fearful emotions. If you *are* ... if who you really are is an enlightened God-self, then what could you possibly fear?"

18.

"Awhile ago, you made it sound like meditation was undesirable. I know from experience, meditation can help you attain spiritual awareness," said Francis, a woman in her fifties, dressed in a bright red suit.

"Buddha said he gained nothing through meditation," I said.

"That's ridiculous," she said angrily.

"You didn't let me finish, Francis. Buddha gained nothing through meditation, but he lost much. He lost his fears. He lost his desires. So you see, we're back to the absence again ... the absence frees your true self, your God-self."

Turning to the other seminar participants, I said, "Excess formal meditation can generate physiological effects that may not serve you. But there are many ways to meditate. Focus the concentration you use in meditation (or hypnosis) upon all your activities to be *in the moment*—to flow. If you're in bed with your mate, be totally with your mate. If sitting at your computer, be at your computer. If taking a quiet walk, be mentally quiet and walk. It's all meditation, and in time it becomes automatic."

"But my mind doesn't seem to want me to be in the moment and flow," said Medina, who started speaking before the support team could run a microphone to her. "I get just a taste of it, and unrelated thoughts come rushing in, pulling me this way and that."

"Right. Because you try to cram so much into so little time, you make yourself neurotic." I smiled at her, "Like not being able to wait to be recognized and given a microphone."

"Sorry. But what can I do about it?"

"Simplify your life."

"That's it?"

"It's a start. You can also make a decision to do only what you're going to do. If you're going to read a book, don't read a book with the stereo or TV on. Don't respond to the telephone. Read in a place others won't interrupt you. Just read. If while reading, your mind intrudes, just say to yourself, 'I'll deal with that later. Right now I'm reading a book.'"

19.

"It's natural to resist when someone is being unreasonable," said Benedict, a man in his mid-thirties clad in a sweater and jeans. "I have a mother-in-law from hell."

The other seminar participants laughed appreciatively.

Benedict grinned, then continued. "As you advise, I remind myself that my expectations are in conflict with what is. But when ma-in-law wheels into my life spewing animosity, I resist what is."

"I can relate to that, Benedict," I said. "I catch myself faster these days. I'm better than I used to be, but I haven't integrated all resistance. I do know that what I resist, I draw into my life. Eventually we integrate fear by encountering it until forced to deal with it by learning *to let go.*"

"I'd like to think I'm learning," he said.

"If you don't learn in this life, you can always reincarnate with ole ma-in-law in your next one."

"Oh, my God. I'm learning. I'm learning."

Returning my attention to all the participants, I said, "While you're learning to integrate fear, remember that life is not something to be endured and suffered through. Life is about achievement and success, love and awareness, joy and exaltation. Of course, no one will force you to experience life the way it is meant to be. You have the free will to ruin it if you want to."

CHAPTER **3**

LIFE ISN'T FAIR

K arma is not a halfway proposition—it is or it isn't. Either life is meaningless, or there is a plan behind existence. If there is a plan, then an intelligence must have created that plan. Call the intelligence God, Universal mind, energy gestalt, collective unconscious, All-that-is, Divine mind, or any other name you want.

If there is a plan, wouldn't justice be part of the plan? But look around. Where is there justification for all the misery and inequality? How can you justify child abuse, mass starvation, rape, murder, war, people ripping off people and seemingly being rewarded for it?

Karma can explain it all. Show me any other religion or philosophy that can. Karma rewards and punishes—a multi-life debit and credit system that offers total justice. Either absolutely everything is karmic or nothing is karmic. Accept or reject the concept of karma, but it is senseless and confusing to accept a halfway position.

My research shows that neither God nor the Lords of Karma bestow your suffering. It is your decision and yours alone to tackle the opportunities you have experienced and are experiencing in your life. You and you alone are responsible for absolutely everything that has ever happened to you. In your Higher Mind, you are fully aware that in order to progress, you must learn.

And the fastest way to learn is by directly experiencing the consequences of your past thoughts, words and deeds.

Q.

I beg to differ with you about karma being the only philosophical/religious concept to explain the injustice and inequality in the world. The Christian Bible says that God works in mysterious ways. And it foretells that those who have suffered will receive their rewards in heaven.

A.

Let's relate that explanation to a common situation. Take the case of two boys born on the same day in different parts of the world. One is born to loving parents. He's healthy, has a wonderful life, goes to college, experiences a successful career, a good marriage and has three neat kids. He dies peacefully in old age. The other boy is born crippled to cold, unfeeling parents who live in poverty. His father deserts the family and his mother dies of tuberculosis, which her son also contracts. Even as a child, he has to work long hours to survive. Suffering from disease, he never marries and dies painfully at an early age in an institution.

How can the life of misery be justified? Does the poor man receive a greater reward in heaven than the man who lived the fulfilling life? How just is that? A rationale such as "God works in mysterious ways" is a cop-out.

If the First Council of Nicea hadn't edited reincarnation and karma out of the Bible in A.D. 325, Christianity could explain the inequality. Karma says that the man who lived the nice life was reaping a reward, while also testing himself in many areas. The poor man chose his lifetime to balance several factors: In a former incarnation he cruelly beat another man, paralyzing his foe's arm ... so he was born crippled. In another past life he was arrogant about his wealth, so he needed to experience poverty to learn compassion for those less fortunate. In the past, due to pride, he refused to accept assistance from anyone ... so in this incarnation, the disease forced him to accept the compassion of others desiring to help him.

Karma Editorial
September, 1993

Here's one of my favorite metaphysical axioms: "You are what you think, having become what you thought." In other words, cause and effect (karma) begins with your thoughts, which are then expressed as words and deeds. Karma means balance and the supreme potential of balance is harmony. So we're all here on earth to attain harmony, and our karma is self-imposed testing to see if we've learned to respond to life harmoniously.

If you're like me, it's difficult to remember this when angry, fearful or lacking confidence. The key is to remind myself that wisdom erases karma. If I've learned wisdom by handling a test harmoniously, I may avoid similar testing in the future.

This is easier said than done, because it doesn't work to repress your emotions in the process. You may hide your fear and develop an ulcer. I think harmony begins with logical understanding: "If I handle this situation harmoniously, my life will get better. If I handle it fearfully, I will generate more of the same. Since it's dumb to create more pain, I'll go for harmony." The logic helps.

Q.

More than any other metaphysical communicator, your teachings seem to be based on the concept of karma. Why do you give it so much importance? And if karma is *what is,* why worry about anything? Why should I watch what I eat? If it is my karma to die at age 45, I might as well enjoy eating junk food up until then. If it is my karma to be crippled in an accident, why should

I bother to wear a safety belt in an automobile? What will happen will happen no matter what I do.

A.

Reincarnation and karma are the basis of reality on the earth plane. This being the case, what understanding could be more important?

In response to the rest of your question: First, I doubt that anyone would be predestined to die at the age of 45. But, assuming this to be the case, maybe in many past lives you've eaten badly, suffering ill health as a result. Hopefully, in this incarnation, you have karmically learned that healthy food will create a healthy body. But you always have free will. If you haven't learned, you may live on junk food and have to once again suffer years of ill health as a result. We eventually learn through our pain, even it if takes lifetimes.

Regarding seat belts: Let's say it is your karma to be crippled in this life, if you haven't learned to protect yourself when given the opportunity. Maybe in many past lives, you'd been foolishly reckless. Now, in this life, you have another chance to see if you've learned from your past mistakes. Karma is a teacher, and wisdom erases disharmonious karma. The root meaning of the word karma is "action." So, have you learned enough wisdom from the past to take the appropriate action in this life?

Declaration of Purpose

In *Master of Life Winners* magazine, this Declaration of Purpose is stated on the table of contents page: "To promote mental, physical and philosophical self-sufficiency. We believe that unhappiness and failure are self-inflicted, and happiness and success are self-bestowed. You can create your own reality through awareness and programming techniques. We are dedicated to communicating Master of Life concepts: a personal philosophy of becoming all you are capable of being, and a perspective of involved detachment in which you accept all the warmth and joy in life while mentally detaching from negativity. We have nothing to join."

Q.

The most interesting passage in your magazine is perhaps the least noticeable: the Declaration of Purpose. After contemplating it, I felt compelled to share my thoughts with you.

The first two sentences seem to me to promote a philosophy of self-centeredness. I agree that we're responsible for our own "karma." However, I don't agree that all unhappiness and failure are self-inflicted, nor that all happiness and success are self-bestowed. Aren't we also affected by our environment to varying degrees?

The third sentence seems to me an invitation to embrace hi-tech escapism. For myself, escapism of any kind is a "nice place to visit, but I wouldn't want to live there." I admit, as a product of the cold war, I fear subliminals. I'd rather do my intentional retraining the natural way.

I find the fourth sentence encouraging through the word "being." I wish you had stopped there because I feel that negativity is necessary. Fear (yin) and love (yang) are both an important part of who we are; but they must balance. To attempt detachment from either pole can only result in an imbalanced personality.

As for the last sentence, having nothing to join: I feel that we are already joined; indeed, inseparable. We were together at the inception of our grand experiment, and when we tire of amusing ourselves with life, we will be together at its completion. I appreciate your departure from structured religious organizations, though.

Please don't misunderstand me. I have a great deal of respect for your wisdom and power. I hope you've found my letter interesting and entreat you to respond.

A.

I contend that karma either is or isn't. There is no halfway karma. This is either a random universe or there is meaning to life. In other words we either evolved out of the sea and our life is the meaningless result of evolution, or there is some kind of plan. My research tells me there is a plan—it's called karma and reincarnation.

If karma is the basis of reality, then everything is cause and effect, and your life is a self-creation (from a multi-life perspective), including the environment of your question. This does not negate free will or your ability to erase karma through wisdom.

The third sentence is an invitation to reprogram your reality through awareness and any techniques you desire, including "hi-tech" tapes, which we offer. "Awareness" is the key word.

A basic Zen goal is to attain "detached mind"—the idea of accepting all the warmth and joy in life while detaching from the negativity by allowing it to flow through you without affecting you. You don't detach out of repression, but out of wisdom. You know that to respond to negativity only makes things worse, so the goal is to become *aware* enough to let it flow through you.

I agree about yin and yang, which is the natural expression of energy. But I teach that you can replace negative expressions of energy with positive challenge, on every level, interpersonal to international. **Example:** Historically, every nation that has reached its peak has fragmented and collapsed when unopposed. Is it possible for our nation to replace cold war opposition with the positive challenge of resolving the homeless, education and infrastructure problems we're currently facing? Of course it is. Doing it is something else.

Q.

What is your view of the karma of those who died and those who lived in the recent DC10 airline crash? (Several letters, including one from someone related to a survivor of the crash.)

A.

I've never found a better answer than in *Many Wonderful Things* by Robert W. Huffman and Irene Specht (DeVorss 1957). The book is based on the past-life regression and channeling experiments of the Boulder Fellowship Foundation that took place in the early 1950s. The book had a major influence on me when I first began to experiment with past-life regression. The following "contact" dialogue is from the book:

Q. When a man has learned his lesson for this time, then God gives him rest?

A. Yes, that's right.

Q. And it could be in an accident that he is killed?

A. Yes.

Q. Perhaps it could be in an airplane accident. We have had so many of them recently—45 or 50 people killed at once. We could assume that each of these people had learned his lesson for this life?

A. Yes, and had created his own situation for death. God does not predetermine accidents. We create our own situations, problems, and deaths.

Q. I would like to get this so that it is very clear. People may possibly think that the airliner's crash was all planned, and that nothing could avoid those fifty people's dying in that crash. Is that true?

A. They feel as though God's hand had plucked it from the skies. But they have created this situation, this learning, this understanding, through their own learning and mistakes. But we make death a horror, a fear, a punishment ... no, no! It is a true and joyous release, and resting time.

Q. We might then assume that, if an airliner should crash today, the people who might die in that crash would be drawn to it?

A. Yes.

Q. But then it would be predestined to crash?

A. They have created that predestiny—not God.

Q. Then if those fifty people had completed their lesson for this time, and had earned their rest, they would be drawn to this airliner, which would crash and give them that release?

A. Sometimes the situation is a learning which has been created. Yes, they would be drawn together to learn together. But God does not predetermine these things. We have done so by our mistakes, our errors, our learning.

Q. Now then, if this airliner were going to crash, then those who were not ready, who had not learned their lesson, would be kept away from it?

A. Yes, yes. It is so complicated to you. Those ones would be what you would call "spared!"

Q.

Are some people predestined to contract AIDS? And what about divine protection in regard to this disease?

A.

Just as with other diseases, some people have predestined their AIDS experience as a karmic balance—especially with the early cases, before there was a general awareness of the disease. The only simple answer is to repeat that karma is always a teacher.

As an example, I am aware of a young man who took his own life in a previous incarnation. In this life, just when he most wants to live, he will probably die of AIDS. His lesson is to learn the value of life.

A man with arthritic hands, learned that in another life prisoners were tortured at his hands. It was his job and he didn't like it, but he subconsciously continues to feel guilty, which manifests in his hands.

Today, rather than all AIDS cases being predestined, it would seem many are cause and effect. In response to your question about divine protection: If you are part of God, you are also God

... thus you are your own protection. Everyone has free will to choose safe sex or abstention. Someone with a karmic history of recklessness might choose AIDS to teach himself that life is precious.

Q.

In a seminar, you said that our glands are "karmically controlled, and a way to trigger balance and learning." Please explain that a little more.

A.

Our glands control what we are. Since everything is karmic, our glandular balance is also karmic. In your body, your glands maintain orderly relations between various systems of the body. Metaphysics teaches that glands are subject to orders from your own Higher Self, dictating what you need to karmically learn.

A couple of examples from the Edgar Cayce readings demonstrate this: Cayce did a reading on a girl who had a shapeless, overweight body due to an imbalance in her endocrine system. Seeking the cause in trance, Cayce saw her as an athlete in ancient Rome who had ridiculed those less agile and graceful than herself. To learn, she had become what she scorned.

In another reading, a man sought out Cayce because a lifelong digestive weakness forced him to maintain a strict diet in order to assimilate food. Cayce perceived two lives of gluttony, one in the court of Louis XIII, the other in Persia. The two lifetimes of excess caused the man to self-create a glandular balance blocking the tendency to overeat.

The latest word on glandular imbalance comes from John Money, professor of medical psychology at Johns Hopkins University School of Medicine. He has treated 30 men with pituitary gland malfunctions who were unable to fall in love. Although they physically enjoyed making love, they were incapable of **feeling** love. According to Money, "The romance messages get blocked. Just as a color-blind person can't perceive certain shades, they've never felt the fire of erotic passion."

Theoretical past-life karma explanations: Someone who claimed great love he didn't feel in order to seduce someone who really loved him. Someone who used another's love only as a means of attaining self-gain.

Q.

Maybe I'm a dunderhead, but there's something about karma which baffles me. If it is true, as you write, that I choose between lives to incur suffering and pain in my life to make up for acts committed in previous lives, then is it not true that I also chose beforehand to live the life in which I committed the misdeeds? It seems that if we choose our path ahead of time and understand the consequences, we would never pick a life in which we inflict suffering on others.

A.

All karma is self-reward or self-punishment, but the goal is always self-testing. You think you've learned your lessons, but you won't know for sure until you test yourself "under fire." As an example, let's say you've earned a reward of wealth and fame. The testing will depend upon how you use it. Actress Ali McGraw lives down the street from me, and she is constantly using her position to help others in everything from local community projects to major programs to get kids off drugs. And I know some famous personalities who use their time and money only for selfish purposes—primarily to buy another line of cocaine. Guess who will probably have more wealth and fame in the future?

Self-punishment is to resolve your karma until you can forgive yourself. But you won't forgive yourself until you know—on every level of your body and mind—that you'll never make the same mistake again. I think we can learn through love and wisdom, but we seem to learn fastest by directly experiencing the consequences of our actions. Thus, we do most of our learning through pain.

Now, to better answer your questions, let me use an example. Let's say that before you were born into this life, you consulted some wise souls on the other side to decide which karma areas you were ready to test. We'll assume that one of your tests will be "relationships." In past lives, you've messed up in this area on several occasions. In Carthage, Pompeii and Rome, you were together with another soul named Aila. In each incarnation, you were cruel and dictatorial to her.

But now many lifetimes have passed, and you're ready to test yourself in this area. To pass your tests, you respond to situations with neutrality, compassion and, ideally, unconditional love. To fail your own tests, you respond with anger, hate, desire to control, or desire for revenge. Remember everything you think, say and do creates karma. And that includes the motive, intent and desire behind everything you think, say and do.

All right, now the decision is made that you and Aila will be born again to be together ... and to see if you've both intuitively learned to respond with love to the situations you'll encounter. You won't be allowed to consciously remember your past, so you're counting on your intuitive awareness to assist you in passing your relationship tests.

Twenty-one years after you were born, you meet Aila. You are both attracted to each other for reasons you don't understand. A few months later you are married. Five years later, Aila— whose name in this life is Mary—has given you two children, and you are both very happy. But in your years together, Mary has had an affair with one of the men she works with. You find out about it. How do you respond? If you choose to respond with hostility, it will probably be the beginning of much misery and you may fail your karmic test.

Subconsciously, Aila is getting even with you for all the repressive past lives you shared, so she may not be doing too well in the karma department. The pendulum of cause and effect is swinging. Of course, one of you may learn your lesson in this life and the other may not. In that case, you probably won't come back together again. Next time, the one who didn't learn will simply find another soul with karmic configurations to match their needs.

Let's carry this a little farther. We'll assume that you are also ready to pay off some karma incurred in a lifetime in ancient Greece. As a jailer, you purposely withheld food from a prisoner you particularly hated. Because you did this, the man died. So, you've chosen in this lifetime to be afflicted with a food problem. With even the slightest nutritional intake, your weight skyrockets. So you are always hungry, always dieting. And the man you once starved is now back in this life as your employer. He has never liked you, for reasons he doesn't understand, and has blocked your promotions, going out his way to discredit you. Consciously, neither of you knows anything about your past-life association. From a karmic perspective, it is just a game to test your levels of awareness.

Q.

If one's karma is the result of what he did or didn't do, then how is one to know which is which? Is he impotent because in his last life, he was celibate (say, a priest) and has carried over that trait into this life or is he impotent because in his previous life, he exploited women and is therefore paying his debt in this life?

A.

This is the kind of question that is ideally answered through past-life regression, for either situation could be causing the problem. Assuming that everything is karmic, and all karma is self-imposed, then the past-life exploitation of women would have to be balanced. But there is nothing as powerful as guilt when it comes to creating karma, and if you subconsciously relate sex with guilt or abstinence with spirituality, the impotence may be self-inflicted as a carryover from the priestly incarnation.

I don't know if you're talking about a real situation or if you're simply using impotence as an example, but here is how I would suggest one deal with any physical problem:

1. Have the wisdom to be medically responsible to the problem by seeing a specialist. It was once believed that impotence was a mental problem, but today it is known that most often it is a physical problem.

2. Attempt to find the cause through directed regression with a hypnotist you trust, or through self-hypnosis/meditation or prerecorded regression tapes, such as my *Past-Life Therapy* album. The Back-to-the-Cause session is worded, "You may go back to an earlier time in your present life, or you may return to an event that transpired in a previous incarnation."

3. Once you know the cause, begin to program self-forgiveness in daily meditation/self-hypnosis sessions. Let your mantra be, "I know the cause, and I now forgive and release myself from the effect." Then begin positive programming. I offer several pre-recorded titles; so do other tape lines.

Q.

You say that 'what is, is.' But you also say that we have a choice of our karmic path. Which is it? If we have karma that we are 'destined to fulfill,' then we don't really have a choice, do we? By resisting, we can, in fact, cause greater pain, can we not?

A.

"What is," is reality. When I say, "Don't resist what is," I am saying don't resist **unalterable** circumstances—don't resist what you can do nothing about. I don't see how that relates to the next part of your question. Yes, you do choose your karmic path—the path that will best allow you to experience what you need to learn. Yes, there may be some predestined events that you will encounter in your life, but again, wisdom erases karma. Edgar Cayce said, "the law of grace supersedes the law of karma." If you give love and mercy, you'll receive the same in return.

You can mitigate the predestined event by how you live your life from the time you're born until the time of the event. The more positive, loving and compassionate you are, the more you may modify circumstances. And the more self-actualized you are, the less meaning any negative event will have.

Q.

I have an awful time accepting the idea of life being predestined, as palmistry and astrology seem to indicate. It's not that I don't believe destiny is what is. But I keep coming back to the idea of "why bother, if my future is already destined to be?"

A.

Many general aspects of our lives appear to be predestined, but our reactions to life are not. You've reincarnated on schoolhouse earth for another opportunity to react to situations of your own creation as a self test. Here you are as God, wanting to grow, so you create games that allow you to learn things. Knowledge equals growth. React harmoniously to the lesson and you've probably learned. React disharmoniously and you'll get another chance to learn the same lesson—probably sooner than you'd like. So maybe life is just about reactions!

Your best mirror for learning to react usually will be your relationships, which reflect limitless possibilities for growth, from petty issues to major insecurities. You may be destined to be with Willie or Wendy, but your potential for happiness is up to you. In the end you probably will find that strong relationships are based upon love, compassion, acceptance, and freedom. The fewer expectations, the better. Weak relationships usually mirror someone wanting the other person to be the way they want them to be.

Q.

Your writings about reincarnation and karma make me crazy. The idea that I might come back with my ex-husband is enough to make me want to kill myself. (But that would just hurry the process, wouldn't it?) Tell me, please, is there a way around it?

A.

No one will force you to come back with anyone. However, when you're on the other side in spirit, you might see things differently. You may decide the fastest way to learn is another round with your ex. In this life, you were probably what I call "Karmic Companions"—two people destined to form a union to confront unlearned lessons from past lives. In other words, conflict was destined as a self-test to see if you had learned to let go of fear and respond unconditionally.

This kind of relationship can be karmically structured in one of three ways: **Locked-In**—the players must remain together to resolve their conflicts; **Open-Ended**—the outcome of the relationship depends upon the growth of the partners. If love matures, they will remain together. But if stagnation destroys the potential for spiritual growth, a parting is assured, and **Destined-To-End** for the growth opportunity the parting provides. Can you and your ex let go with love, without excessive hostility, anger, and desire for revenge? If not, a future mating is likely.

Q.

I'm worried about creating bad karma the way I'm using one of your *Silent Subliminal* tapes. My husband watches three or four hours of prime-time television every night. I use a small auto-reverse tape player to play the "Male Virility" tape all evening. (I erased the first minute of the tape where you list the subliminal messages.) I know I'm being manipulative, but his lack of sexual interest is a problem for us. He says he wishes he were more turned on, but if he knew about the tape, he'd probably get mad.

A.

Karma gets tricky when it comes to motive, intent and desire. Why isn't your husband turned on? Maybe the problem is too much TV. If I watched four hours of TV a night, I'd be a vegetable.

Subliminal programming to "buy a new Honda" would not influence Cadillac owners to buy a Honda, but they might start thinking about buying a new Cadillac. Relating this to your situation, if your husband isn't interested in you sexually, the programming may be charging up his libido for another woman.

CHAPTER 4

THE POINT OF POWER IS NOW

Editorial
September 1994

A hand-lettered Seth quote taped above my computer says, *"The point of power is now."* It's something I need to be regularly reminded of. In other words, the past and future are not factors in controlling your destiny because it's right now. Reality is manifesting at a point where your beliefs intersect with the physical world. Change a belief now and you automatically alter the past by viewing it differently. The changed belief also alters the future by creating new potentials.

Beliefs have influenced the choices (actions) that have shaped your life. Reality is defined by actions, and until you act, life is theoretical. With each act, you hope to improve your chances of getting what you want. Knowing that *the point of power is now*, you can use this awareness to alter beliefs that aren't working for you, then act in accordance with your goals. If "goals" sounds too structured, think in terms of desired outcomes in the key life areas: 1) attaining your objectives, 2) fulfilling the responsibilities you've accepted, 3) obtaining the responses you desire from others, and 4) finding personal peace.

Hypnosis or meditation are effective ways to reprogram a

negative belief with a postive belief. In an altered state, chant a mantra that summerizes your goal. Visualize your desire as an accomplished fact. Give yourself positive suggestions worded as if the goal were already attained. Examples: "I always finish what I start." "I am self-reliant, self-confident and filled with independence and determination." "I openly discuss my needs."

I'll sign off with another favorite quote: They asked Buddha what time it was and he said, "Now!"

Satori Seminar
Belief Talk and Process

Change results from the acceptance of new beliefs. Psychologists, psychiatrists, hypnotists, human-potential trainers, and brain/mind researchers agree that beliefs are the basis of individual reality. Beliefs generate your thoughts and emotions, which create your expriences.

If you aren't happy with your current life and want to change it, you must change beliefs, which are not hidden deep in your subconscious mind; they are part of your conscious awareness, but you view them as attitudes, assumptions, or facts.

Your reality is the manifestation of your core beliefs, which includes your relationships or lack of relationships, and the fact that they are harmonious or disharmonious ... your level of success ... even the physical state of your body.

Once, while conducting this seminar, an overweight woman stood up, put her hands on her hips and said, "Richard, I'm overweight because I overeat, not because of my beliefs."

"But it is your beliefs that cause you to overeat," I responded. "And if you want to lose weight, you'll have to change your beliefs. Hundreds of companies offer weight-loss tapes—hypnosis, sleep programming, subliminals, which are quite effective. And they're all structured to help you do just one thing: program new beliefs into your subconscious mind."

I asked the woman what went through her mind when she

observed a woman with a beautiful body. Without hesitation, she replied, "All beauty and no brains."

"Really?" I said.

"It seems to be true," she said.

"You will always live up to your self-image," I said. "If your core belief is that having a beautiful body means you would be brainless, you'll subconsciously never allow it to happen."

The overweight woman looked at me quizzically and sat down. In an attempt to assist all the participants to become more aware of their unexamined beliefs, I asked them to finish a sentence in their mind. And I want you to do this too. Without thinking about it, just finish this sentence: "I think wealthy people are ..."

In the seminars, over half the participants will come up with responses such as, "unhappy," "dishonest," "snobs," and "thieves." Such negative responses exposed their deep-seated beliefs about wealth.

"You also can't become what you resent," I explain. "If someone driving a Rolls Royce pulls up beside you at a stoplight, and you look over and respond negatively to this symbol of wealth, your resentment is blocking your own quest for riches. You will always live up to your self-image even if it works against you."

Back to how you finished the sentence: If you have a core belief that becoming wealthy means being dishonest or snobbish, you'll never allow yourself to attain wealth. Even if you should attain it in a windfall, such as a lottery, you will not allow yourself to retain it. Statistics support this by showing that most lottery winners quickly go through their winnings and find themselves back where they started.

Maybe you finished the sentence with a word like "lucky" or "blessed." But that doesn't work much better, because since you're not wealthy, you're not lucky or blessed.

Here are some additional sentences to finish that will provide you with a quick general belief check. I want you to mentally finish the following incomplete sentences. Read and respond instantly, the way you really feel, without considering how you "should" feel. Note if your response is positive or negative, and mentally flag those that generate an emotional response.

My diet is ...

My current weight is ...

Daily exercise is ...

People with beautiful bodies are ...

When it comes to dietary self-discipline, I ...

Eating only healthy foods is ...

When it comes to addictions, I ...

People are over the hill at the age of ...

The older you get, the ...

Being older means ...

Marriage is ...

Having an affair is ...

Money is ...

My potential for success is ...

When it comes to ambition ...

My creative ability is ...

My ego is ...

Happiness is ...

You have the idea. Think about how you finished some of the questions, and consider those keeping you from being all you can be.

Your subconscious mind is a great memory bank containing every thought, word and deed. It has a record of what the doctor delivering you said at your birth, what you did at your fourth birthday party, what you thought after your first kiss, and what you had for lunch on September 23, 1982. Your subconscious functions as a computer, but like a computer it lacks the ability to reason; it functions only as the result of programming. Thoughts, words and deeds are the "belief software" that generate your thoughts and emotions, in turn creating your future experiences.

If your subconscious were to receive no new programming, it would continue to operate on past input. This, of course, cannot happen, for you are constantly feeding new programming or data into your subconscious mind. Every thought and deed programs you, but your thoughts must precede your deeds, so the real power of programming is in your thoughts. If your belief software is self-limiting, your experiences will be self-limiting. If it is more negative than positive, you are programming a negative future reality.

In the '50s and '60s, medical doctors, such as Maxwell Maltz, began to explore the power of the mind. Many universities conducted experiments, and brain/mind researchers began to report on the power and limitations of the subconscious. They discovered three critically important truths that are the basis of all self-change programming.

1) Like a machine, your subconscious is incapable of caring whether you get what you want out of life or not. It works impersonally—whether for or against your conscious desires—as the result of programming.

2) The subconscious mind cannot tell the difference between fantasy and reality, a real experience and a vividly imagined experience. This means it can be tricked with visualizations and properly phrased suggestions.

3) Although the subconscious mind doesn't reason, it does seek to logically correct itself, much like an error-checking computer program. Once it has accepted new internal programming, it begins to generate circumstances that will align your outer life with your inner beliefs. So, if you properly program your desires, your subconscious mind automatically begins to bring them into reality.

After deciding what you want out of life, the next most important step for self-change is to begin monitoring your thoughts. This is a lot easier than it sounds. The idea is to simply catch yourself whenever you think negatively about anyone or anything. When you recognize mental negativity, say to yourself, "positive opportunity." Then replace the negative thought with a positive version of the same thought. Rather than repressing negativity, this technique reprograms beliefs that are not serving you.

Q.

In one of your books you say, "Belief doesn't work!" Buddha said, "Do not believe, for if you believe, you will never know. If you really want to know, don't believe." Later, under the Law of Manifestation, you refer to belief with a different definition: "Everything manifest begins as a thought, an idea. Ideas and experiences create beliefs, which in turn create your reality."

The Virgo part of me is distressed by the lack of clarity on this point.

A.

I am referring to belief in two contexts. First, I urge you not to blindly accept concepts but to experience them. As an example, many people believe in reincarnation. They think it's reality. They may even be willing to stake their lives on it, but it's a belief and they don't really know. Myself, I've researched and experienced reincarnation through hundreds of regressions and verifications and cross-check experiments until I'm no longer coming from a position of belief. I'm coming from experience. I know reincarnation and karma are the basis of reality.

In the second context, I'm referring to beliefs as programming. (The Satori Seminar Process at the beginning of this chapter demonstrated this aspect of belief in detail.)

Q.

How can you say, "Truth is not something you find, it is something you create"? Truth is! There is but one Truth. All the teachings, self-improvements, awareness, just lead us closer to that inner reality.

A.

Bhagwan Shree Rajneesh said, "Start fresh: a clean slate with no belief, with no dogma, with no faith. Then there is a possibility that you may find what is the truth. And the truth is neither Hindu, nor Mohammedan, nor Christian. And the truth is not in the Bible, nor in the Koran, nor in the Gita. The truth that you will find—you will be surprised—is nowhere written, cannot be written. It is impossible to write it. It has never been uttered by anybody and it is not going to be uttered by anybody."

You are confusing facts and truth. A fact is something that has been objectively verified. But my truth is not necessarily your truth. Zen teaches that truth cannot be taught. It is something that is discovered within your own soul. Buddha and other mystics taught that truth arises from the deepest source of your being.

Q.

I have read your books, as well as those of many others. Try as I will, I still have doubts about metaphysical teachings. What do you suggest to help me get past this?

A.

Continue to doubt, because there is much more power in doubt than in belief. When you believe, you stop seeking the truth. Truth is what works, and you'll find out what works through direct experience. Then it is no longer a belief, but a reality.

Energy Editorial
April 1988

Those close to me know I'm big on the subject of energy. I'm always asking myself and others, "Do you really have the energy for it?" (referring to a new project or direction). I know that if you do have the energy and are clear on your intent, half the battle is already won. And if you don't have the energy, there is little chance of a winning effort. You'll soon lose interest and put the project behind you, usually losing self-esteem in the process. A couple of years ago, Tara said to me, "I think it's time you wrote another book for Simon & Schuster Pocket Books. With their distribution, it could introduce hundreds of thousands of new people to your work."

"I just don't think I have the energy to make a mass-market title successful," I replied. "My first books for Pocket are filled with the enthusiasm of self-discovery, that's what made them so successful. You can't fake that. A reader always perceives the author's sincerity and energy." But I thought a lot about Tara's words.

I then took some of my own advice. In my seminars, I've told thousands of people, "Don't assume there is only one way to attain your goals." After 18 years of investigating past lives, I'm very objective; it's difficult to get excited about even the most interesting cases, but I asked myself, "What part of your metaphysical investigation is most exciting?" The answer was easy and the same as when I'd written *You Were Born Again To Be Together*, the idea of romantic love spanning lifetimes.

"What would really challenge you regarding your work?" I asked. "To stretch my abilities as a writer," was another easy answer. That did it. I'd found my energy. I had gathered some wonderful, documented case histories over the years and I decided I'd write about them in a totally different way—in third person. This was a new and different challenge and it generated very high energy. Could I communicate the true cases in a short-story format that would read quickly? Could I incorporate metaphysical philosophy without slowing it down? Could I make it work?

When my editor read my first case history, she cried. I knew then that the answers were yes, yes and yes. I had the energy and I knew Pocket Books would go for it. *Predestined Love* sold extremely well for six years.

Q.

What is your feeling about goals?

A.

I'm fine with goals, although I'm personally more inclined to target a strong general direction than a specific goal, because I don't want to limit the power of the Universe. People often commit to goals before committing to a process that will move them toward the goals. Before concentrating on your goals, concentrate on a process that is natural for you and one you will enjoy.

Using myself as an example: My primary process is writing about metaphysics, but the words can be used in many different ways: articles, books, seminars, tapes, et cetera. There is no way to describe the joy I experience in this. I would sit in front of my computer for eighteen hours at a time if Tara and the kids didn't come and get me. It is something totally natural for me, substantiated by astrologers who tell me this dharma is in my chart. Tara is an excellent palmist and she claims this destiny is in my hand "loud and clear."

"What if I'd wanted to do something else?" I asked her.

"No way," Tara replied. "You're here to do what you're doing. Nothing else would have worked out as well."

Q.

In a seminar, you once conducted an altered-state session about role models. I awakened surprised to find I had modeled my life after a high school hero. Can you repeat the premise of that process?

A.

People invariably choose role models, usually while still in early high school. The choice is made with little conscious awareness about how much you imitate and mimic them. This could be someone in school, a family member, a public figure ... anyone. The role model becomes your self-image. You go through life making small decisions as if they were not part of any master plan, as if all along you were responding to individual circumstances. The truth is, there is a master plan. You set it into motion when you chose your hero.

The key questions in the process: 1) Think back to your teenage years. Who was your role model? 2) How has your role model related to your life? 3) Has this worked for you? If not, has it worked against you? 4) How might your awareness of your role model affect your future? 5) Could you pick a new role model that would better serve you in the future?

Q.

Your goal-accomplishing ideas seem to me to generate competition, a concept I feel needs to be eliminated if we ever hope to spiritually evolve.

A.

Can't we spiritually evolve while accepting "what is" about human nature? Competition drives people forward in every facet of life. To resist it is to resist life. As I write this, I have only to look back on the last four hours of my life to see several positive examples of competition.

For lunch, I had a chicken salad at the McDonalds down the street from my office. The man eating next to me had a McLean sandwich (90 percent less fat than a regular hamburger). I don't think Ronnie McDonald would have offered either of these healthy options if it weren't for the competition. They've also stopped frying foods in lard and are using more expensive vegetable oil because of competition. Their ecologically incorrect styrofoam food packages have been replaced with paper. Because of competition.

After lunch, I took my son Hunter to his tennis lesson. Initially, I was teaching him to play, but I knew he needed the competition of his peers to be challenged to improve.

Following Hunter's lesson, I met Tara at the courts, and we played two sets. We originally took lessons together, and the sport became one of our favorite shared activites. Over the years we've gone back and forth at being the better player. Tara rapidly improved last year, often beating me by embarrassing scores. So I went back to mind programming and analyzing my game. I found too many unforced errors and realized I was trying to play Jimmy Conner's game to my detriment. I made a grip change after reading Ivan Lendl's book and developed a new game model.

Competition caused me to improve and within ten days I was beating my wife more often than not. Now Tara is gaining again. I suspect she's channeling some Wimbledon champion on the other side. So, I had better get out on the courts and spend more time practicing with the ball machine.

Please understand, we do this out of fun, not fear. We applaud each other's good shots, and although our friends laugh, we always kiss as we change ends.

Q.

How do you find the courage to do what you dream of doing when fear holds you back? I know you say that courage is a matter of being afraid and acting anyway. But that doesn't resolve it for me.

A.

You're not alone. Most people allow fear to keep them from making growth choices, or they find security in their insecurity and never act to fulfill their dreams. In some cases this might be a wise decision, but more often than not, by keeping one foot in the safety zone, they will never know their full potential for joy.

There is no magic answer to your question. Life is a matter of choices. You'll find the courage to make it or you won't. And while you're deciding, consider this quote by Anais Nin: *"Life shrinks or expands according to one's courage."*

Q.

What is the primary problem you encounter in working with people who aren't as happy and successful as they desire to be?

A.

Two things: 1) **Lack of clarity.** They don't know exactly what they want. 2) **Self-deception,** which manifests as, limiting beliefs, resistance to what is, faulty assumptions, assumed limitations, or irrational (often selfish) viewpoints.

Q.

I'm attractive, warm, friendly, and I want a one-on-one relationship. I date, but it never seems to work out for long. Is it me? Is it my karma? I know dozens of people in the same boat. How can I create my own relationship reality?

A.

If we could sit down together, I would ask you four questions:

1) Is there a hidden payoff in remaining single? Explore this by considering all the changes that will take place in your life when you find a mate. Which changes won't you like? Examine these changes closely for they may point to a subconscious block.

2) Do you know how to give? I know people who claim to want a relationship, but they're takers—"me-me people" who talk endlessly about themselves without showing any interest in others. Giving is also a matter of showing respect. Yes, everyone operates in their own self-interest all the time. But there are two kinds of selfishness: "piggy" selfishness and the selfish aware-ness that you must give to get in life.

3) Are you realistic? I know a 43-year-old woman who constantly complains about not dating. She is only attracted to men in their late twenties and early thirties. There is certainly nothing wrong with the older woman/younger man scenario—but it limits options. A good-looking, successful man of 58 asked her out, and she was offended at his nerve in thinking she might be interested in him. Another realistic point: If you're waiting for a burst of "soulmate fireworks" to identify a potential mate, know that it seldom happens. Take a chance, get to know them, give love the space to grow.

4) Are you doing something about it? Read books on the subject. Do mind programming with pre-recorded hypnosis tapes. Be creative in deciding how to meet eligible people, then go where they are.

Everything is karma, so your current circumstances are the result of attitudes, actions or inactions in the past. But the point of power is now. Get clear on your intent, explore any blocks, be ready to give of yourself, be realistic, and start acting.

Q.

Why am I always attracted to the wrong kind of men? Is it my karma? Did I do something wrong in a past life that is forcing me to go through all this pain?

A.

You are picking the wrong kind of men to teach yourself not to pick the wrong kind of men. It's called learning through pain, which is the way most of us learn—suffering as the source of awakening. The alternative is to learn through love and wisdom. But that might be too easy.

Q.

I've been working with many different brands of weight loss and prosperity tapes with no success. My profession as a teacher is slowly but surely killing me and the stress is causing high blood pressure. My psychic development has stopped. My spiritual growth has been at a standstill for several years. I am tired of being depressed, overweight, professionally unhappy, dissatisfied and spiritually stagnant. Can you suggest any methods that will help? I've been to hell and back and I'm tired of merely existing.

A.

Your letter is typical of many I receive every week. You want a magic solution instead of confronting the real problem. Why would you remain in a profession that is causing you high blood pressure and "surely killing" you? Is money and security that important, and what value will it be if you're dead? Your weight problem may be directly tied into your unhappiness, and how are you going to attain any prosperity if all your energy is drained by the repressive job?

I am reminded of the metaphysical man who believed that the Universe would support him in attaining his desires. So he sat on the edge of a cliff, and called out to the Universe, "Support me, Universe." And the Universe answered, "How can I support you with your ass firmly planted upon the edge of the cliff? Once you jump, I can support you!"

What about jumping? What is the worst that would happen if you simply walked away from your job tomorrow? You might starve, but I doubt it. You could always move to Spider's Breath, Montana, and cut logs ... and wouldn't that be better than "merely existing?" Sure, you might have to lower your standard of living, but you'd probably have so much more enthusiasm for life that you would soon resolve the rest of the conflicts.

In regard to the self-programming tapes: Don't use several different brands on the same subject. They could easily contain conflicting suggestions due to the way the ideas are phrased. Also, tapes are powerful supportive programming, but you have to do your part. You have to be clear on your intent and willing to make changes in your life. If you're using a weight tape, you must diet. The tape will assist you to stick to a diet of healthier food. And it will work better if you first resolve the all-consuming occupational crisis you've been experiencing.

Q.

You say, "Stop asking 'why' questions." I find that ridiculous. Being logic-oriented, I need reasons for everything.

A.

People always act emotionally. They invent logical reasons to justify their actions to themselves and others. Yet these reasons are merely rationalizations and rarely have much to do with facts. The reasons don't matter, and no one could possibly know what they are. They're buried in your viewpoint, which is the result of all your past experiences.

When you ask "why," you demonstrate your lack of awareness. When you explain "why," you demonstrate your lack of awareness, and you give away your power, which reduces your self-esteem. You do what you do because you do it. That's why. They do what they do because that's what they do. That's what is.

You do need to distinguish between 'why' questions intended to take away power and 'why' questions intended to clarify. "Why didn't you call last week?" is a manipulation. "Why is it better to use no-lead gas in my car?" asks for clarification.

Q.

I'm very attracted to someone in my company, although I'm afraid of him and don't understand why. Do you think it could be based upon a past-life tie?

A.

Maybe. But first I'd consider some other factors. 1) If you're normally not fearful of others (and especially if you're somewhat psychic), you might be perceiving his insecurity and fear. 2) You may simply fear his rejection. 3) There may be something about him that triggers a subconscious fearful association—maybe from your childhood. 4) You're in awe of him, and he could be reflecting unintegrated admirable qualities within yourself (the "mirror"). 5) It could relate to a past-life relationship.

CHAPTER **5**

LETTING GO

*"Not only has one to do one's best, one must, while
doing one's best, remain detached from
whatever one is trying to achieve."*
— *Janwillem van de Wetering*

*"Attachment is the great fabricator of illusions; reality can
be attained only by someone who is detached."*
— *Simone Weil*

The dreaded **ego** is nothing but the expression of fearful emotions, and the spiritual concern with the need to repress this abstract aspect of your totality is the ultimate ego trip. Instead, concern yourself with detaching from fear-based emotions. As you succeed, your ego will diminish all on its own.

Examples

1. You brag to your friends about your promotion at work. An expression of ego? No, an expression of fear. You fear you're not important enough, and the promotion validates you.

NOTE: The purpose of 99 percent of your conversation is to attain sympathy or boost your importance. Knowing this, maybe you don't need to say it!

2. You tell your lover how to do something. When he doesn't take your advice, you get mad. An expression of ego? No, fear.

Your lover's independence challenged your need to be right.

NOTE: Everyone is subconsciously programmed to be right. Instead, let the other person be right, and concentrate upon winning the game.

* * * * *

In his book, *Waking Up—Overcoming The Obstacles To Human Potential,* Charles T. Tart says, "Some paths are powerful, some may have been effective in the past but no longer work, and some are dangerous. Some are dangerous neuroses disguised as paths. All genuine paths require courage: courage to buck the social tide, courage to see yourself as you really are, courage to take risks."

* * * * *

The Zen goal of detached mind is viewed from a different perspective by Charlotte Joko Beck, who teaches at the Zen Center in San Diego. In her book, *Everyday Zen,* she dialogues with a student, "I don't think that we ever let go of anything. I think what we do is just wear things out."

Detachment sounds good, and self-actualized people claim to be able to do it, at least to a degree. But most human beings lack the ability, because they lack the awareness. Instead of detaching, they just wear things out. They get obsessed with old pain, or a person, an idea, or a desire ... and they play it, and play it, and play it until they wear it out ... or they act on it ... or they make themselves crazy.

Maybe you've ended a relationship or watched others end one. At some point it gets clear that both people want to part. Although they're both overwhelmed with anger and are clearly "over it," they can't let go. They stay together ... and talk about it ... and talk about it ... and beat each other up about it ... until finally, they wear it out to the point they can let go.

Instead of going through this pain, accelerate the process of detachment by realizing your thoughts are not reality. Become an observer of your thought processes, and stop judging and labeling the other person. Simply let the thoughts roll through your mind as if observing a TV show, and remind yourself that the thought is the result of old programming, but it isn't you.

Q.

In the seminars and in print, you say, "There is nothing to seek and nothing to find ... so look within." Please explain more.

A.

That's an abbreviated bit of Zen. Many seekers drift from one organization to another in search of enlightenment. Today, some channeler has the answer. Tomorrow, it will be a new guru. The more the seeker searches, the more frustrated he becomes, because he is looking outside of himself for the answers.

You are a spiritual being. This means that beneath all your layers of subconscious fear programming lies an enlightened soul and total awareness. What you seek is already there. It's like digging a well. The water is already beneath you. All you have to do is remove the layers of dirt and rocks to access the water. You must simply remove the barrier between yourself and what you desire.

Granted, it isn't as much fun to pursue internal awareness as it is to have someone else offer you magical answers. But someone else's answers are not your answers. Meditate and read everything you can. Attend many kinds of seminars (as long as they don't want you to join anything), and decide what you need to change about yourself. Then create your own reality, using all the tools at your disposal.

Q.

It seems to me your path of spiritual revolution lacks love!

A.

To attain **True Freedom,** you have to free yourself from the repressive aspects of society, religion and government, none of

67

which want you to be free. Society wants you to wear its approved masks of dress and behavior. Religions want you to believe and contribute as they dictate. Government always seeks greater control of your life.

True Freedom is freedom **of** the self and **from** the self. Begin your personal revolution by freeing yourself from your past programming. Then you must decide what you want—not what your mate, boss, society, or religion wants you to want—what do **you** want? You have a divine right to experience joy. In my seminars, I have the participants consider doing only what they enjoy in life. And that's just the beginning of the revolution.

In regard to lacking love: Unconditional love is not a heart-felt emotional love for every single person on the planet, outwardly expressed as an "I love everybody" mask. The concept is fostered by cosmic foo foos and gurus claiming such love as proof of their enlightened status.

Unconditional love is the acceptance of others without judgment, blame or expectations. That doesn't mean you stop thinking and evaluating. It means that you accept others as they are, without expecting them to change and be what you want them to be. I accept the cosmic foo-foos as they are. I think their lives would work better if they were grounded, but that isn't a condition of acceptance. And unconditional love is about loving yourself first. If you can't love and accept yourself, you can't love and accept others.

Q.

You seem to advocate that everyone accept everyone else exactly the way they are. That just doesn't work in life. We all try to influence each other.

A.

You cannot successfully force another person to change and become what you want them to be. To do so would only cause someone to repress who they are, and no one can successfully repress for long without experiencing adverse mental/physical effects.

But when it comes to influencing others, we all attempt to do this all the time. Almost everything you say to other people is an effort to influence them, even if only to influence them to listen to you. Attempts to influence are only wrong when you conceal your efforts or coerce your will with threats, manipulation or physical force. You must always leave it up to the other person to change because they want to change.

Q.

For someone who claims we need to rise above judgment, you seem pretty judgmental about a lot of things. How do you explain that?

A.

Spiritual people so often get stuck on this concept. You need to resolve 1) judgments based upon your expectations, 2) judgments which result in trying to change someone else, 3) judgments generated by fear-based emotions. These judgments echo your ideas of right or wrong, your desire to control, and your fear issues.

Rising above judgment doesn't mean you stop deciding what does and doesn't work for you. There are only so many hours in each day, and if you're intelligent, you will spend what time you have efficiently and pleasurably. If I said, "I don't want to spend time with Ralph, because I don't enjoy his company," you probably wouldn't have a problem with the statement. But if I said, "Ralph is a braggart who dominates every conversation," you'd accuse me of being judgmental. But that's why I don't want to spend time with Ralph. I'm not judging him to be wrong for being a braggart, but I know it's wrong for me to spend time with him. Referring to points 1 and 2 above: I don't expect him to be anything other than what he is, and I have no desire to change him.

Q.

In a seminar, you said, "What you deny to others will be denied to you." Will you better explain that, please?

A.

You always experience what you deeply believe to be so. That being the case, what you feel strongly or emotionally about creates your reality. If you resent other people's success, you will be denied success. If you're disgusted by someone else's sexual enjoyment, your sexual experiences will become disgusting. If you're jealous of another's loving relationship, you will be denied an ideal relationship.

The purpose of karma is to teach—in this case, to teach us not to judge. But don't misunderstand my response. I said, "what you feel strongly or emotionally about." To decide not to pursue monetary success because it might complicate your nice, simple life is not "resenting" someone else's success. To decide a particular sexual practice doesn't work for you is not being "disgusted" by another's practice.

Q.

I remember a "soap opera" process you used to conduct in the Bushido seminars. Would you please recap it?

A.

Life is a soap opera. Everybody has a soap opera—a sad tale they repeat to everyone willing to listen. Here are a few examples:

"I'm underpaid and unappreciated." "My mother-in-law runs my life." "My husband's kids by his first wife are incorrigible." "My husband is an S.O.B." "I've got bad astrology—my Aries doesn't line up with my wife's Pisces." "My wife doesn't understand me." "My hemorrhoids are acting up again." And so on. Some people even broadcast their soap operas on personalized auto license plates: IN DEBT. LOSER. SAD SAC.

Everybody has a soap opera. When does yours get aired? What do you talk about? Who's your audience—your mate, friends, co-workers, relatives, strangers? What is your victim story? Martyr story? Rightness story? Think about it. Boil it down to one short line. "My soap opera is ..."

After some powerful group processing, I point out that every time you repeat your soap opera, you are programming the complaint into your subconscious mind, giving it more power.

Q.

Some of your tapes are for "personality transformation." That's ridiculous—no one can change their basic personality.

A.

Not unless they want to. Your personality is the sum total of your past programming and the interaction of three factors: traits, viewpoints and habits. None of these three are inherited. They are acquired, thus they are alterable through effort or programming.

Habits are simply repetitive actions, such as the way you drive to work or the way you dress in the morning.

Traits are distinguishing characteristics, such as always being immaculately groomed, or always exaggerating your accomplishments.

Viewpoints are the way you look at what happens to you and your specific attitudes toward life.

The desire to change your personality must come from within as a result of realizing that what is isn't working. What habits are negatively programming your reality? What personality traits are working against you? Which of your viewpoints are programming disharmony? You need to be very clear about what you want to become. That's when programming will be effective.

Q.

You say, "What you resist, you become." I don't like bigotry, and when someone uses a racial slur, I believe in speaking up and attacking it. Does this mean I'll be a bigot in a future life?

A.

Usually, I phrase the statement, "What you resist out of fear, you become." In other words, if you resist gays or straights; or Arabs, blacks, whites; pro-life or pro-choice women, and you can't learn to integrate such prejudice, you are expressing fear. You're here on earth to learn to let go of fear, so if you need to become what you resist in order to learn, then you will.

In regard to resisting bigotry, karmic consequences only result from negative attachment. To understand that others do not necessarily reflect your level of awareness and calmly state your position is one thing; to experience intense anger and "attack" (your word) the racial slur, is something else. Attacking with anger is fear. You want to control the way the other person thinks, which is not your right.

Q.

Please clarify what you mean when you say, "Let anger pass through you without affecting you."

I have learned that when anger is not expressed properly and effectively, it can stay trapped inside and cause future problems. I find that I've reached a point where I refuse to get angry at anything 98 percent of the time; when I do get angry, I feel completely fatigued afterwards. I also find that I'm misdirecting my anger toward the wrong people. I have a feeling that my mental and physical lethargy is due to not knowing how to handle this emotion.

A.

When you feel anger you should express it, not repress it. But how do you express it? Screaming, threatening and throwing things is one way. Saying, "What you did really hurt me and I need to let you know," is quite another.

But let's go back to basics. You feel anger because you aren't getting what you want: approval or control. Simplified, this is a matter of your beliefs or expectations being in conflict with what is. You expect the other person to be the way you want him/her to be, but that's not what is, and you suffer because of it. Can you change that person? No. So you might as well accept what is and let go of the anger.

Your choice is to let go or not let go. Either way, it won't change what is. If you don't let go, you only make matters worse by mentally programming negativity, which will have to be balanced in the future. The only intelligent choice is to let go.

Change has to start intellectually and work its way down to the emotional level. Next time you find yourself getting upset, say to yourself, "I'm upset because my expectations are in conflict with what is." This will help diffuse the anger, because you'll have to question your right to have such expectations. At the same time express your angry feelings, clearly, without emotion.

In time, with practice, you will begin to allow anger to pass through you without affecting you (without repressing), because it is the most intelligent choice.

Some additional notes on anger: **Active anger** is expressed directly to the source of the problem. **Passive anger** is expressed by punishing someone without confronting them. **Consciously unexpressed anger** is withheld because we feel it is in our best interest—maybe to be polite or avoid a confrontation. The result is resentment. **Unconsciously repressed anger** is turned inward, which becomes depression.

Q.

Would you share again what you discussed in the Whole Life Expo workshop about letting go of our attachment to bad experiences?

A.

Good things can have bad outcomes. Bad things can have good outcomes. Rather than panicking or rejoicing, *wait and see:*

When a man won the lottery, his wife decided her share of the windfall provided the money to leave him and start anew.

A corporate officer attained a major promotion and a big raise, but her new responsibilities gave her ulcers and grey hair.

Twelve years ago, a friend contracted Reiter's disease (a severe arthritis-like disease). He was in bed for a year, but the disease strengthened his immune system and he recovered. Although he has been HIV-positive for ten years, his strong immune system has protected him from any T-cell decrease or the onset of AIDS.

A woman who had a car accident met her husband while recovering in the hospital.

After spending most of his adult life working as an electronic specialist for a major corporation, a man lost his job when the company closed down. He moved to Lake Arrowhead, California, and started a home-security alarm business. Today he makes a lot more money and prefers his mountain lifestyle.

Don't try to second-guess the universe. Things happen because they are destined to happen—to get us from here to there, so we can resolve our karma and fulfill our earthly purpose.

Q&A

While conducting a seminar in San Francisco, a female participant told me she would prefer not to know anything about karma. "Knowing that even my thoughts are creating karma is overwhelming," she said and sighed.

"And the motive and intent and desire behind your thoughts," I added.

"Even worse," she said. "If I didn't know these things, my life would be easier."

The incident reminded me of the story of an Eskimo hunter who asked the local missionary priest, "If I did not know about God and sin, would I go to hell?"

"No," said the priest. "Not if you did not know."

"Then why," asked the Eskimo, "did you tell me?"

... which reminds me of another story in response to some recent letters. For those who need a "cosmic sign" to point the way, I love the following, reported in Charlotte Joko Beck's *Everyday Zen*:

To avoid the rising water during a flood, a man climbed up on the roof of his house to await rescue. Eventually a rowboat arrived and the rescue team shouted for him to climb into the boat.

"No, no. God will save me," he said. "I'm praying."

The water rose higher and higher until it covered the man's legs. Another rowboat happened by and they tried to coax him into the boat. Again he said, "No, no. God will save me. I'm praying. I'm praying."

When the water had risen to the man's neck, a helicopter arrived and hovered above him. The rescuers shouted, "This is your last chance, grab the ladder."

"No, God will save me," said the man as his head slipped beneath the water and he drowned.

When he got to heaven, he said to God, "Why didn't you try to save me?"

God said, "I did. I sent you two rowboats and a helicopter."

CHAPTER 6

WHEN ALIVE, BE COMPLETELY ALIVE

Stopping at a newsstand on Sixth Avenue, a derelict approached for a handout. "Get out of here, I'm working this side of the street," screamed a cripple, sitting nearby in a distorted position on the sidewalk.

"Screw you," mumbled the beggar.

"Nobody says 'screw you' to me!" raged the cripple, leaping to his feet and busting an ivory-handled cane over the derelict's head. No one said a thing. The not-so-crippled cripple went back to the sidewalk, sadly examining his broken cane. The beggar, his head bleeding, moved on in search of a meal ... past a guy peeing in the street ... past girls with purple hair ... past a black man with a sheet over his head, dealing Thai-stick. I bought my copy of the *New York Review of Books*. It was a nice Friday afternoon in Greenwich Village, New York.

Tara and I were in the city for a week to conduct three seminars. We spent the afternoon shopping, and while my wife tried on outfits in the Village shops, I thought about the two beggars. In regard to defending their turf, they were no different than the gangbangers in Los Angeles or any other major city.

To refuse to meet a gang member's eyes, or to look at his girlfriend, or to enter his territory might *dis* (as in show disrespect) him enough to initiate retaliation.

Novelist Robert Parker says, "If there are no things which are important, then things are assigned importance arbitrarily and defended at great risk. Because the risk validates the importance."

Something has to matter in your life.

If you're busy raising a family, the tasks keep you focused on your priorities. If you're building a business, you have to concentrate upon the most important aspects to assure success. If you have an interesting career and a circle of exciting friends, your calendar is probably overflowing with things to do. But if nothing of importance is going on in your life, maybe someone stepping on your sneakers is enough to cause you to fly into a rage.

In a New York seminar, I processed a woman who spent her life suing people—lots of people.

I asked her to explain, and she proceeded to relate all the fights, feuds, and lawsuits she was involved in. As she talked, her monotonous voice became aroused, her eyes lit up and her body language transformed.

I said, "You attract the people and the problems, because they create the aliveness you're otherwise lacking."

"That's not true," she said. "I hate it."

"Bullshit! You love it. Look at you! Just telling us about your problems has transformed you into a vibrant, alive human being."

"That's absolutely ridiculous," she said, scowling.

"Are you married? Do you have many close friends?" I asked.

"No and no. So what?"

"Do you love your job?"

"Not particularly."

"What do you do for excitement?"

"I like metaphysics, but my problems with people take up all my time."

By this time, the seminar participants were howling. After a little more processing, the woman admitted to us and to herself that she did indeed "enjoy the hell out of the conflicts." I rested my case.

Positive aliveness accomplishes the same internal purpose as negative aliveness, and it's a lot more constructive.

When nothing is important, we have to make something important.

Marianne, a single female friend, was extremely upset by the thoughtless actions of a neighbor in her condo complex. Weeks later she was still dwelling on the slight. Marianne has very little going on in her life and is frustrated by her lack of a relationship and an unfulfilling job.

When nothing is important, we have to make something important.

When my son Scott was ten years old, my mother came to visit for two weeks during an uneventful time in her life. One afternoon, while knitting, she burst into tears for no apparent reason. When asked why she was crying, she said, "Scotty is such a willful child. When he's old enough to drive a car, it's going to be terrible."

When nothing is important, we have to make something important.

If your life is filled with worthy goals, satisfying relationships and exciting activities, you probably "don't sweat the small stuff." But if nothing **is** of importance, and if you're getting upset over things that really don't matter, it is time to consider some new and meaningful activities to generate aliveness.

Q.

In the Albuquerque seminar, I was surprised to hear you promote "challenge" as spiritually desirable.

A.

I teach that "aliveness" is critical to your mental, physical and spiritual well-being. Aliveness is the exhilaration that makes you feel glad to be alive; the joy, stimulation and pleasure that makes life worth living. The way to experience aliveness is to add challenge to your life. This will usually result from wise risk taking.

Science has proven that matter is energy, and that energy cannot die—it can only transform. Energy must also move forward or backward; it cannot stand still. If moving backward, it is preparing to transform (reincarnate). Since you are energy, you are also moving either one way or the other. Challenge creates aliveness, which moves energy forward.

Q.

What about negative aliveness? I think it's what I'm doing when I have short, secret sexual affairs.

A.

Aliveness is part of it, but there's another factor to consider. Your mind wants to feel good right now, and when you let it control you, it will choose immediate gratification at the expense of long-term satisfaction. You need to realize that only the result immediately following the act matters as far as your mind is concerned. The second consequence (marital problems or divorce) doesn't matter. This is because you're being directed by an unconscious computer-like mind that doesn't reason, it only responds to programming. Your behavior is mentally programmed by the initial reinforcement—in this case, aliveness, excitement, sexual release—and it programs similar future behavior.

This works positively as well as negatively. So you have to learn to override your mind by keeping your personal agreements.

Aliveness Editorial
May 1993

"Don't ask yourself what the world needs. Ask yourself what makes you come alive, and then go do that. Because what the world needs is people who have come alive."—Howard Thurmon, an African-American preacher in San Francisco. The words are a powerful way of stressing the importance of "aliveness."

Few people experience aliveness very long or very often. Those who don't know aliveness usually wait for life to provide a wake-up call before venturing into new directions that offer exciting potentials.

"Should I give up my job and move to Arizona?" "Should I end my relationship?" "Should I commit to him?" "Should I gamble on doing what I really want to do?" "Should I take this risk?" "Should I tell her what I really feel?"

We fail to act out of fear, desperately attempting to maintain control so there is no chance we'll be rejected, surprised, or fail. By keeping one foot in the safety zone, we eliminate any chance of real aliveness. What about being afraid and acting anyway? What about being a hero or heroine? Heroic stories are always about a protagonist who ventures from familiar territory into a fearful situation, which he or she faces and conquers before returning home with expanded awareness.

We all have the potential to create our own reality. We just have to be a hero or heroine to become the person we wish to be.

Negative Aliveness
Seminar Dialogue

"My primary fear is that my husband will have an affair and leave me," Joyce said. She was in her mid-to-late thirties, attractive and casually dressed. Holding the microphone, she wound her long brunette hair around the index finger of her free hand.

"Do you know the cause of the fear?" I said.

Joyce shrugged, met my eyes. "We see a lot of people socially. Every time Luke meets an attractive woman, I think, 'this is the one.'"

"And how does this fear manifest in your life?"

"Manifest? You mean arguments?"

I nodded.

"Well, when I voice my fears, he gets mad. He says I don't trust him, that I'm holding his one affair against him. Five years ago he had a fling at a convention in Toronto."

"And he told you about it?"

Nod. "All about it. I was upset, but at the same time I ..." Her eyes dropped.

"Felt excitement?"

Nod.

"Negative aliveness. What you fear also thrills you, causing a surge of adrenaline. This kind of excitement can be addictive, resulting in behavior that incites the fear. Tell me about your fights."

Joyce's eyes looked up and to the left, indicating she was accessing memories. "Last week we attended an opening at a Santa Monica art gallery. We were introduced to a lot of people, and Luke was a little too responsive to a blonde wearing skin-tight leathers."

Joyce lowered the microphone, tapped it a couple of times, took a deep breath, then said, "On the way home, I told him it bothered me. He was shocked by my reaction."

"Can you recall your dialogue with Luke?"

"I asked him what he would have liked to do to the blonde. He said, 'Nothing.' I said, 'Well, that's not true, you're a man. Any man would like to have sex with a woman like that.' And he said, 'Sure,' but that he wouldn't, because he loved me. And I said, 'What if you had my permission, then what?'" She paused.

I waited.

"So he told me and I got upset. But when we got home, we made passionate love." She looked away at some of the other participants, then back to me. "Maybe it has become addictive, because I can see the pattern."

"Anger followed by an adrenaline rush. Then, a week or two

weeks or a month later, you do it again to attain another shot of adrenaline?" I said.

"Wow, yeah."

"And behind it is the fear of abandonment."

"I've viewed it as possessiveness," Joyce said.

"And to further complicate matters, you're probably still angry at Luke for having the affair and angry at him for having the power to fuel your fear."

"I have a right to be angry."

"People only get angry when they don't get what they want, Joyce. In your case you wanted your husband to be faithful, to control his actions."

"I don't think it's as simple as not getting what I wanted," she said, irritated.

"It's that simple, but there are three steps. 1) Luke had an affair; 2) You believe he betrayed you; 3) You got angry. Step two, the expectations resulting from your beliefs, sets up the effect."

Joyce didn't respond.

"Do you believe he betrayed you?"

Nod.

"What else do you believe about what he did?"

"I believe he put my feelings second and that it was a real slap in the face. But I guess betrayal sums it up pretty well."

"Can you recall a time in your past when someone else betrayed you?"

Joyce lowered the microphone, stared at the floor, then finally met my eyes and shook her head.

"Would you like to explore it with regression?"

"If you think there's value in it."

NOTE: Participants in some seminars are conditioned to respond instantly to altered-state suggestions. This allows me to individually regress participants quickly into their past, either back to an earlier time in this life or to a previous incarnation. A support team member assists in the process and the participant is usually regressed while standing.

I touched Joyce on the forehead, activating the post-hypnotic suggestion, counted her down into the altered state and gave her the following suggestion:

"You are going to go back into your past to a time you were betrayed, if such a situation actually transpired. On the count of three you'll be there. One. Two. Three. Tell me what you see and what you are doing."

Joyce's face contorted; she looked like a sad little girl. She hesitated then, in a child's voice, yelled, "My daddy lied. HE LIED!" She started to cry.

"Tell me what happened."

"My daddy promised he would come to my Christmas program, but he didn't come. And he doesn't come home anymore either." Crying.

"What's your name?" (The question was to make sure the current lifetime was being explored.)

"Joyce."

"Why doesn't daddy come home anymore, Joyce?"

"He fights with mamma all the time, and now he doesn't come home."

"All right. What would you like to say to your daddy right now, if you could? You don't have to worry about being punished for it. What would you really like to say?"

Joyce sniffled, scowled, then screamed, "I HATE YOU, DADDY. I HATE YOU. YOU SHOULD HAVE COME TO MY CHRISTMAS PROGRAM, AND YOU SHOULD COME HOME. I WISH YOU'D DIE. I HATE YOU." Sobbing.

The female support team member put her arm around Joyce, supporting her.

"Is there anything else you want to say to your daddy, Joyce?"

Sobbing, "But I really love my daddy too."

"I know you do. When mothers and fathers don't get along, it isn't anyone's fault. The relationship just isn't working. There may have been valid reasons why your father didn't come to your program and why he separated from your mother. Do you think you can find it in your heart to forgive him? Really forgive him?"

There was a long silence, Joyce stood with her head bowed, deep in trance. Finally, she nodded.

"Then tell him you forgive him, Joyce."

"I forgive you, Daddy. I love you."

"I couldn't hear you, Joyce."

"I forgive you, Daddy. I really do."

"I still couldn't hear you, Joyce."

Yelling. "I FORGIVE YOU, DADDY. I LOVE YOU AND I FORGIVE YOU."

"All right, let's come back to the present, Joyce. You're leaving the past. On the count of three, you'll be back in the present. One. Two. Three. And now I'd like you to forgive Luke for having an affair, if you can find it in your heart to do so."

After a long hesitation, she said, "I forgive you, Luke. I wish you hadn't done it, but you came back to me and I know you love me, and I forgive you."

After awakening Joyce, I asked if she felt better.

"Much better, like a weight has been lifted."

"You probably never mourned the childhood betrayal, which added fuel to Luke's actions."

"I don't think I could have recalled that situation on my own, and if I had, I wouldn't have given it any power," she said, shaking her head. "Mom and dad separated for several months when I was about seven, but they got back together and are still together."

"You still need to integrate the fear of abandonment. The first step in resolving a fear is to identify it—to stop denying it. You've done that. Your fear is being fed by the belief that Luke might have another affair and leave you. This is a potential, but it's probably a faulty belief that is keeping you from confronting the fear. How else could you confront the fear?"

Joyce hesitated, then said, "Trust my husband. Don't ask for reassurance."

"Good place to start. Your asking for reassurance gives him power. I don't think we ever get rid of fears, but we can integrate our fears by changing how we view them or by deprogramming them."

"Deprogramming them?" Joyce said.

"You are not your fears, not your thoughts. Accept that your thoughts are not reality. The next time you find yourself fearful about Luke, just become an observer of your thought processes. The more you do this, the faster you will desensitize the fear and the less it will affect you. Life gets better in direct proportion to our ability to increase harmony and decrease disharmony."

"So when I see Luke flirting with a blonde, I just observe my reactions?"

"Observe your inner dialogue: *'Well, there's Joyce being possessive of her husband again. Luke is enjoying the company of another woman. It doesn't mean he's going to sleep with her. Joyce assumes he's got better taste than to do that.'* You get the idea. You're not Joyce, you're the observer observing Joyce's issue. The thoughts aren't you, they are the result of old programming. The technique can help you attain clarity and accelerate the integration process."

"Anything else?" Joyce asked.

"Regular mind programming with hypnosis (tapes or self-hypnosis) is powerful. And you can apply the 'mirror' to any situation. It says, 'that which bothers you in someone else is something you recognize in yourself.' In other words, what you fear Luke doing is what you desire to do yourself. Would you like to have an affair, Joyce?"

"No!" She scowled at me.

I waited without responding.

She looked away, rolled the microphone, adjusted her blouse.

"Well, sometimes I fantasize about it."

"Would it be to get even or enjoy the attention of another man?"

Joyce started to answer, then stopped. Shrugging, she said, "I don't know. I'm no longer upset about Luke doing what he did, but I'm really tired of being afraid he'll do it again and maybe leave me."

"Joyce, unless you integrate your fear, it has the potential to destroy your marriage."

Nodding, she said, "If I had an affair, Luke might leave me."

"Or you might fall in love with your new lover and leave Luke." I paused. "An affair doesn't sound like a very good idea if you love Luke."

"I love him very much. We've been together nine years and have two beautiful children."

"So why not do everything you can to integrate the fear and free yourself **from** yourself?"

She nodded, smiled, counted on her fingers. "1. Forgiveness; 2. Be an observer; 3. Trust my husband in vulnerable situations; 4. Don't ask for reassurances; 5. Mind programming."

"Each time you trust your husband, you'll realize that you've survived and become a little stronger."

"Thanks," she said, handing the microphone back.

Q.

You write about aliveness and the idea that we are here on earth to learn that life is to be enjoyed. I have a hard time with the "joy" part. It seems to me that having enough food, clothing, shelter and the hope of buying a new car is about as joyful as it gets.

A.

Joy doesn't result from having things. I find it in the process of creating and in my relationship with my wife, children and friends. I also find joy in personal accomplishments and in the accomplishments of others responsible for creating exceptional music, art, writing, film, architecture and dance. At the risk of sounding corny, I have to admit to finding joy in the smell of the morning air when I go out to pick up the newspaper.

Q.

I get confused about the concept of enlightenment. You seem very Zen on the subject. Enlighten me please.

A.

Zen Master Nansen suggested that enlightenment is not anything beyond the world. "Those who are enlightened 'liberate' themselves not from the world but from their own deluded minds, which force metaphysical distinctions upon the world. If it is a cow, it is a cow; if it is a moon shining through the window, it is moonlight."

Joshu is my favorite Zen Master (China, A.D. 778-897). A monk once asked him, "To be holy—what is it like?"

Joshu replied, "To dump a mountain of shit on a clean plate."

In Zen language that means if we do not divide the world into "holy" and "unholy," there is nothing to stain it.

Q.

You say, "Change takes time. But I think enlightenment occurs in an instantaneous flash of awareness.

A.

Attaining enlightenment is like tearing down a cage. When the walls of the cage are down (fears integrated), you have more freedom, but you soon realize there is another, larger cage awaiting you. When you tear it down, there will be another. It is a step-by-step process and the more self-actualized/aware/enlightened you become, the less you will be affected by negativity. The journey itself is empowering. And the journey is a critical part of the process of liberation.

Q.

I recently read some of your literature, and I am astonished by your audacity. As for myself, I am an evolving spiritual being, living high in the desert in solitude and earthly tranquility. I have no desire for fame nor riches, and unlike you, I have no motive to teach others how to think—nor do I have the nerve. I realize that all acts carry a degree of moral responsibility, and I am trying not to accumulate more of it than I can deal with in this, my (hopefully) final incarnation.

Those of us who have looked at physical existence realistically do not desire more lives, no matter how privileged. Are you there yet? If not ... how do you presume?

A.

What if no one were willing to speak up and share what they know? There would be no books, including metaphysical books. You've read "some of my literature." Not my books, and I assume you've never attended my seminars.

The question to ask yourself is: "Am I wasting an incarnation?" I teach that we're all enlightened Masters of Life beneath our fear programming. Yet you're so afraid of involvement and of generating more karma that you live "high in the desert in solitude."

This fear alone may bring you back again and again until you deal with it. Teachers have always spoken of learning to "be in the world but not of it"—to be fully involved in life while consciously detaching from the negativity.

Q.

Exactly what is the Higher Self?

A.

Higher Self is the all-knowing level of superconscious mind and a conduit to the totality—the collective unconscious, the akashic records, the energy gestalt we call "God," and the awareness of all that has ever been, all that is, and all that can potentially be.

Q.

You and many others say, "We are all one!" Obviously, we are all individuals, not one.

A.

There are many ways to view the concept of oneness, but I'll share my favorite: Within Higher Self is the "collective unconscious"—the collective awareness of mankind, all souls, living and discarnate. Thus we are all connected and the living result of this awareness. We are all one.

Although most of us are not yet able to maintain extended contact with this level of our totality, if we are open, we can be influenced. This explains why historically, writers, philosophers and inventors have come up with the same concepts or discoveries at the same time. In these cases of simultaneous discovery, mankind has experienced the prerequisite awareness necessary for the birth of the new idea. So the idea is there, just waiting for discovery by those most attuned to the particular field of vibration.

Q.

Your Bushido Training logo displays a monk holding a sword and riding a lion. It doesn't seem very spiritual to me. Exactly what does Bushido mean?

A.

The symbol is my interpretation of Manjusri, the Bodhisattva of wisdom riding a lion, holding a sword of wisdom that cuts through delusion. Bodhisattva is a Sanskrit term meaning one who supports others in achieving enlightenment. The symbol of karma is a sword. Bushido is a mentally independent and spiritually powerful way of being. In the context of my communications, Bushido is a Master of Life viewpoint and an attitude of detachment attainable by those who seek to transform the way they experience their lives. There are seven basic Bushido principles: 1) Right attitude/detachment; 2) Bravery; 3) Universal love, benevolence and compassion; 4) Right action; 5) Sincerity; 6) Honor and glory; 7) Devotion and loyalty.

Q&A

The following is a conversation that took place between Tara, me, and a friend named Cole, who believed his spiritual quest should allow him to transcend worldly concerns.

Cole said, "I've dedicated my whole life to studying spirituality, but I'm constantly distracted by day-to-day crap. My car needs a valve job, I need to see a dentist, I have arthritis in my foot, and I'm behind in my rent. Don't I deserve some special consideration from on high?"

"Even the most self-actualized man in the world is going to sweat in summer and shiver in winter," I said. "His toothache will hurt terribly, and he will eventually grow old, maybe helpless, and die."

"But if he's enlightened, shouldn't he be capable of detaching from such things?"

Tara laughed and said, "Maybe, through the total acceptance of his experiences."

"Huh?" Cole said.

I responded, "By becoming absolutely at one with circumstances, one paradoxically becomes free of them. When you're hot, be completely hot; when cold, be completely cold; when alive, be completely alive, and when dying, die thoroughly ... to quote Zen."

"That sounds like double-talk," Cole said.

"I'll tell you a Zen story about at-one-ment with circumstances," I said. "When a young monk saw his revered master murdered by thieves, the master screamed out in pain and fear. Because of his master's reaction, the young monk doubted the validity of Zen and considered leaving the monastery.

"Upon hearing this, another master confronted the monk saying, 'Fool! The object of Zen is not to kill all feeling and become anesthetized to pain and fear. The object of Zen is to free us to scream loudly and fully when it is time to scream.'"

Images & Experiences
Editorial—July 1992

Our past programming is what gives meaning to our experiences and generates the mental images that cause us to respond in a particular way. During three weeks this spring, I experienced several situations of spontaneous crowd reaction, a phenomena that always fascinates me.

For my birthday, my son Scott and his wife Sheila took Tara and me to a Bob Dylan concert. When Dylan appeared on stage playing "Like A Rolling Stone," the audience jumped to their feet. To me, the song conjured images of the unrest and turmoil of the sixties and seventies, Vietnam, protests, riots. When the concert was nearly over, "Highway 61 Revisited" generated a spontaneous rush to the stage. Dylan's second encore was "Blowin' In The Wind." As hundreds of people held lighted matches in the darkness, Dylan seemed to symbolize a shared journey we had all survived and were just now celebrating.

The concert took place in Hollywood a few days after the Los Angeles riots. As a people, it doesn't appear that we've come very far in the last twenty-five years. Like you, I watched the riots on TV in disbelief. And I wondered about the mental images that were generating the reactions of those looting, burning and murdering—images of alienation, anger and frustration. I had to explore my own reactions—a mixture of empathy and anger, which I attempted to channel into nonjudgment.

My six-year-old son Hunter knew they were burning his city. I'll never forget him standing in front of the TV set, tears rolling down his cheeks, saying, "I want them to stop." Hunter will probably never forget the images he saw during those four days—blacks as villains, soldiers as heroes patrolling the city streets in assault vehicles. Tara and I have tried to help him understand, but words have limited power. Your experiences equal your programming, which in turn equals your responses ... unless, because you are concerned about the karmic implications, you consciously decide to mentally wrestle with and take control of those responses. It's a concept a six-year-old can't grasp, and most adults never think to question.

The weekend following the concert, Tara, Hunter, our four-year-old daughter Cheyenne and I drove to Edward's Air Force Base to watch the space shuttle land. Hunter's been showing intense interest in anything to do with space, so I promised we'd go see the next landing. Standing on a rise in the desert with hundreds of strangers, a double sonic boom hammered us in the chest, announcing the arrival of the shuttle diving out of the sky. It landed smoothly, and as the parachute deployed, everyone watching broke into spontaneous applause. Tara said, "What a rush!" I nodded in response. For me, the experience was intensely emotional, and I felt a surge of national pride—images of the accomplishments and the good things our country stands for.

Maybe "Schoolhouse Earth" will always be in upheaval to provide us with abundant opportunities to learn to integrate our fear-based emotions, act with unconditional love, and learn to be all we can be. But in the end, no matter what our mental images, each of us has the free will to choose how we will respond to our experiences, whether it's rushing the stage at a concert, applauding the arrival of the space shuttle in the desert, or judging other human beings whose actions we can't understand.

Q.

In the Satori Seminar, you said something about mental and emotional disorders being the result of a collapse of energy. Can you explain that?

A.

You are energy, and physicists tell us energy can't die, it can only transform. And energy can't stand still, it must move. When you are moving in the right direction, life works. But when you're moving in the wrong direction or not moving at all, then life starts collapsing. Neurosis is a collapse of energy. When you don't know what to do, where to go, what to be, a vacuum exists within you and the result is anxiety, phobia, depression. I encourage you to get involved in life, find challenges that will result in aliveness ... which will drive the energy forward.

Q.

The Eastern idea that nothingness is desirable is very confusing to me. "Emptiness is bliss" is another way I have heard it phrased. Please comment on this.

A.

In the sense you refer to, emptiness means unoccupied, at leisure, relaxed, non-desiring, and in the moment. When your mind is not preoccupied with things, you are open to expanded awareness.

Q.

Rupert Sheldrake's latest brain/mind theory says that it's easier to learn something new if it has already been learned by others, the reason being that a resonant field is established by cumulative experience. Can you fit this into your metaphysical philosophy?

A.

As we spiritually evolve, we move deeper and deeper into our center, which is the level of the "collective unconscious;" at this level, we are all connected—all one. So when others know how to do something, the awareness is within us too.

Q.

In a workshop, you said we couldn't have everything we wanted. Somehow, you related this to life areas, goals and values, but I can't remember why you put this restriction on potential.

A.

There are four basic life areas: relationships/family, career/success, social/community, and spirituality/religion. There is no way to become all you can be in all four areas. If you balance your time between the four, I doubt you'll become an outstanding example in any one area.

One of the key success factors is to concentrate your powers. "By zeroing in on a few targets and concentrating your efforts, you create tremendous forces that act to accelerate success," says Joseph Sugerman. I agree, and it starts with aligning your goals and values, which will help you attain clarity of intent.

Q.

I'm disturbed by the idea that pursuing pleasure and avoiding pain will cause me to become numb to pleasure. It's a no-win situation, so why pursue the good life?

A.

If you take drugs or smoke grass, in time, it will take a higher quantity/potency to experience the same effect because you develop a tolerance. It works the same way with addictive pleasures. Once you experience the pleasure as an "effect," you want to possess it and experience ever-increasing levels of intensity. But the predictable result is a tolerance or boredom that amounts to losing the pleasure.

The pleasure could be mountain climbing, a lover, a job, clandestine sex ... anything you deeply desire. When the pleasure fades, the un-self-actualized response is often to "change," to throw away the old and get a new one. The long-term result of this over-stimulation is the inability to joyfully experience anything.

As an example, with a new lover you passionately pursue pleasure. Like an addict, the more you get, the more you want. But more of the same soon becomes less. And the frustration of less generates subconscious resentments, which leads to conflicts. So the repeated pursuit of pleasure becomes the pursuit of pain for anyone unwilling to accept the inevitable changes in a relationship.

Self-actualization is the only solution. The way out of the predicament begins with how you view life—to see yourself and your experiences as cause, not effect. Refuse to be a victim and willingly accept accountability. With self-actualization comes clarity, compassion, the acceptance of "what is," and the release of expectations.

Self-actualization doesn't just happen. You have to passionately desire it, and work to attain it. Actualization means to make something real through action. These efforts can generate the experience of mastery and power. This esteem/security allows you to accept being the cause of your circumstances, making it easier to maintain balance.

Q.

I've tried subliminals, carrying crystals, and many other techniques to develop my psychic abilities, without success. I experienced it once or twice, but never consistently. What do I do? (Condensed from a three-page letter explaining all attempts).

A.

You mentioned everything in your letter but **practice.** To develop psychic abilities takes practice, just like learning to play tennis takes practice. You have to do it, over and over and over again, week in and week out, and you slowly improve.

Sure, subliminal tapes can support your goal, just like subliminal tennis tapes support that goal. But there is no substitute for regularly getting out on the court.

Q.

In the New York seminar you said, if we know who we really are, all problems become simple decisions that need to be made. Relating that idea to my experiences was an eye-opener. Can you elaborate?

A.

As you integrate your fears, you get to know the loving soul beneath your programming—your true-self or God-self. For a person without fear, it would be easy to view problems as decisions that need to be made. You'd make the most appropriate decision based upon your core values and in keeping with unconditional love.

Few of us are at this stage of evolution. We're still hooked on beliefs about how other people and the world should be. As a result, we view our problems as problems and resolve our difficulties based upon who we think we are, not upon knowing who we really are.

CHAPTER 7

SEXUAL INFLUENCES FROM PAST LIVES

Research Project

This multi-issue series was originally published in *Reincarnation Report* magazine. The research goal was to explore the source of sexual problems, preferences and practices. To obtain the information, Bushido Training seminar participants were asked to fill out an extensive sexual questionnaire. I received over 1,000 responses from those who experienced hypnotic regression back to the cause of their sexual "issue." In about half the cases, the participants found the cause in their current life. This series focused only upon past-life causes. The stories are in the participants' own words. Some of the most interesting cases I worked with individually, conducting in-depth regressions for additional information.

PART 1: ADULTERY
Dana

Age 33, some college, artist, married, heterosexual orientation. Subject of search: Occasional adultery, lack of sexual desire and reason for bondage fantasies.

Regression: "I was about 14 years old. It was 1904 in San Francisco. I went to a Victorian house for work as a serving girl to support my sick mother. The house was a bordello. I was sold to a guest of the house without my knowledge. When I served him tea in his room, I was locked in by the man, beaten and raped repeatedly. He was ugly and extremely obese. Later when I was released to go downstairs, the other girls in the house laughed at my discomfort and assured me of a good life and lots of money at the house. I stayed to help my mother because she was ill, never telling her the truth. I felt shame and I didn't seem to like men.

"This I feel is my problem today. I resent having to have sex so often with my husband. I want a more spiritual love between us. I always want my sexual encounters to be fast and done with as soon as possible. This past life makes me feel funny inside! I think 'shame' is the word I'm looking for."

My response: Karma is generated by strong feelings, such as shame, guilt and rage. There are some obvious cause-and-effect patterns between the two lifetimes. As an unwilling whore in a bordello, Dana felt powerless. Today, she has secret bondage fantasies. In the past life, Dana's relationships with men were negative and strictly physical. Today, she resents her husband for wanting a physical relationship. "I always want a more spiritual love between us." And finally, as a whore, her only self-identity was created through sex with a variety of strangers. Today, she may still be seeking the lover who will value her for more than her body.

On a scale of 1 to 10 she rates her current sex life as a 5 and rates her ability to honestly communicate her sexual desires/ needs to her partner as "poor." She feels she is not matched at all with the sexual attitudes/desires of her husband, but she says she will remain in her present relationship indefinitely even if it never changes. She desires sex two to three times a month. Her husband desires sex "all the time."

Katie

Age 39, some college, secretary, divorced, heterosexual

orientation. Subject of search: A pattern of desiring to be unfaithful and excessive adultery.

Regression: "I was a very young Indian girl, probably of high nobility. And the day of my wedding, I saw my present-life lover as the chieftain in full ceremonial costume and wearing a feathered headdress. He was standing next to me as we were married. We were very happy. In the next scene, I was on a mountaintop, where I saw myself crying because he was killed in battle. I was thinking sad and bitter thoughts, wishing he would return so that I could tell him that I was carrying his child. The place was Mexico and the year was 1733.

"I am pregnant in my present life. It just occurred to me that I am punishing my current lover by telling him that I don't know who the father of the baby is."

My response: Feeling abandoned in the Indian incarnation, Katie is getting even by sleeping with a number of men. In refusing to reveal the father, her current lover is denied the experience she was denied in her former life.

Katie's questionnaire shows widely varied sexual experiences. She has desires to experience consensual adultery, group sex, bondage, and exhibitionism. She says that she is stopped from fulfilling her desires by her upbringing and that she considers herself "a nice Catholic girl." She rates her sex life as 7 1/2 on a scale of 1 to 10 and feels that she is totally honest with her partner about her sexual needs. Katie is willing to remain in her present relationship forever, but says she doesn't think she will be happy with her lover in the future. She desires sex all the time, while her partner desires sex only some of the time.

Craig

Age 35, college graduate, advertising executive, married, heterosexual orientation. Subject of search: Excessive adultery, excessive desire.

Regression: "I was four years old. My name was Raquel. My mommy made me sit in a small blue chair at the edge of her four-poster brass bed and watch her have sex with many men who were not my father. I was supposed to hold my doll and be very quiet and watch her. She told me I would grow up to be just like her. My father was away a lot and my mother continued these activities all the time he was gone. We were Lithuanians living in France, and the year was 1890. My mother died when I was 20 years old. My father was away at the time. She was in bed with three other men, urging me to join them, when she turned blue in the face and choked to death. The men all ran away. I didn't tell my father about anything, just that she died in bed. I went into a convent where I became a nun and remained a virgin until I died."

My response: When faced with a cathartic experience, our survival instincts often demand a fight or flight response. As Raquel, Craig chose flight to a convent, where he didn't have to confront his disturbed feelings. In this life, he may be unconsciously choosing to fight by expressing his repressed feelings as excessive adultery.

Craig indicates a wide variety of sexual experiences and desires experiences with a threesome and group sex, consensual adultery and homosexuality. He says that he has not pursued his desires because he is afraid of losing his current relationship and also fears that he might like these activities so much he would give up everything else.

Second Regression: "I was a young boy named George. I was a beautiful child with a very high and sweet voice. I sang in the choir in England. The choirmaster had me castrated before I reached puberty to keep my voice from changing. I was then continually abused sexually by the choirmaster and three of the older choirboys. One of the boys was my brother. I died very young in that life. I think it is interesting that in this life I am always castrated in some way by every woman I have a relationship with. This keeps me from giving 100 percent to any relationship because I know they will end up screwing me."

My response: Maybe Craig felt cheated out of sex in his past life and is making up for it today. He rates his current sex life, on a scale of 1 to 10, as a 4, and feels that he is only fairly well-matched with his partner and that he is just short of honest in communicating his sexual desires and needs. He has wanted his sex life to be other than what it is "for as long as I can remember." He is not sure how long he will remain in his present relationship if his sex life doesn't change; he is contemplating a trial separation. He desires sex every day but his partner desires it only once a week.

Vikki

Age 22, some college, fashion designer, married, heterosexual orientation. Subject of search: Desire to be unfaithful, occasional adultery and the reason for feelings of neglect.

Regression: "I was in a place called Tyros (Ed. note: Tyre was the seaport center of ancient Phoenician culture). The year was A.D. 572. I was married to a military man of considerable political importance. We were down by the water where he prepared to sail on an expedition to Morocco. I begged him not to leave, because I didn't feel it was necessary for him to go. I thought it was pure ego assertion on his part and I couldn't understand how he could leave me. I was very angry when he left, but these feelings lessened with time. I began to have an affair with his brother, who was much more sensitive and understanding of my needs. I wasn't sure when my husband would return and so I became terrified when I found myself pregnant by his brother. I knew when my husband returned, he would have no reservations about killing us both. I ran away to a place that was sort of like a convent, and spent the rest of my life in seclusion."

My response: Each life contains essentially the same experiences. In her former life, however, Vikki responded to the experience with flight. She never resolved her feelings of guilt, anger or being neglected. Today, she has set up the same opportunity to grow, but is again avoiding direct confrontation by blaming her husband.

Vikki indicates on the questionnaire that she has already gratified her desires for adultery and will remain in her present relationship indefinitely. She values her spousal commitment. On a scale of 1 to 10 she rates her current sex life as a 9, and rates her ability to honestly communicate with her partner as just short of honest.

Donald

Age 29, some college, tool-and-die operator, single, heterosexual orientation. Subject of search: Desire to be unfaithful, lack of sexual enjoyment, and the reason he was mated with an inadequate sexual partner.

Regression: "I was a warrior or mercenary soldier in the Middle Ages. I'm not clear on the date. I was married to several women, but not at the same time. Each wife I married would sicken and die a short time later. Sadness always followed the passing of each one. I would become very anxious each time this happened, and I always found a new partner as quickly as possible. This resulted in several unhappy relationships. Life seemed to be a long search for happiness. I despaired of ever finding someone that I could be happy with, even though I was never alone. I finally let myself be killed in battle.

"In another life I was a wealthy Chinese landowner in A.D. 1278. I raped several of my women servants, because my wife was very cold toward me. I blamed the women because sex did not feel as good as I wanted it to. This became a desperate search which resulted in impotence. I treated the women very cruelly, and I think I even killed some of them. They had no defense because I was wealthy and they were dependent on me for everything. My main problem today is finding and establishing a relationship with a woman who matches my level of body, mind and spirit."

My response: In both past lives, Donald searched outside himself for someone to make him happy. When his wives failed to meet that impossible expectation, he blamed them rather than looking within. In the second lifetime, he experienced this blame as anger and cruelty. The effect today is his desire for "excessive adultery, prostitution and kinky sex."

What he really means is, "My main problem today is finding and establishing a relationship with a woman who will make me happy." Until he learns that no one outside himself can make him happy, Donald is doomed to frustration.

Donald does not feel that his attitudes and desires match his current partner's at all, and he rates his current sex life as a 5. He will not remain in the relationship very long if his sex life doesn't get better.

Common Factors

In each of the cases, the primary past-life influences were fear-based emotions: shame, guilt, anger, blame. These emotions carry a psychic charge that must be discharged before the influences will disappear.

For example, Dana, who was ashamed about being a whore, will have to resolve her shameful feelings before she can improve her sexual relationship with her husband. Vikki, who felt neglected by her military husband, is manifesting the same emotions with her current husband. Donald blames his many former wives for not making him happy. It's no surprise he isn't satisfied with his current relationship.

Your Karmic Choices

None of these cases would have been possible without one essential ingredient: blame. Blame means that you don't have to be responsible for your experience.

Each of the subjects feels victimized by the influences of the past. But you can choose *not* to be a victim. First, by acknowledging that you set up your current experiences as an opportunity to learn. Second, by confronting the lessons with unconditional love.

To confront your lessons, be willing to explore and expose your emotions and beliefs about the lesson. For example, if you have a strong desire to commit adultery and it isn't acceptable in your relationship, there's obviously a lesson to learn. Don't assume that the lesson is "Thou shalt not commit adultery." The lesson may in fact be, "I must learn how to communicate honestly with my partner."

The only way to discover the real lesson is to fully experience how you feel about the subject. We'll use adultery as an example. Really experience how you feel about adultery. Allow every feeling to be valid. Remember that no thought is unthinkable.

Explore the emotions that come up for you. Is there fear, anxiety, excitement, resentment, appropriateness? All these feelings are clues to what you really want to learn about adultery.

Next, explore your beliefs about adultery. Do they conflict with each other? Do they serve your best interests? Have you carefully chosen your beliefs, or have you passively absorbed them from the church and society?

Once you've completed this process you'll probably experience one of two results: 1) By exploring your beliefs and emotions without resistance, you've lessened their power and attractiveness. 2) By acknowledging what you really feel and believe, you recognize the appropriateness of your desires.

The next step, if you are currently in a romantic relationship, is to make it all right for your partner to do the same process. Once you've both completed it, take a deep breath and discuss it. You may consider this step risky. It isn't. What is risky is burying your desires until they explode at a highly inappropriate time. By honestly communicating with your partner, you give him or her the opportunity to grow with you. You may even share the same fantasies and not know it.

The worst that can happen is that your partner will be

completely threatened by your feelings and beliefs. Be sensitive to this. Allow your partner time to adjust to new parts of you. Be supportive of your partner without invalidating what you've communicated. Be aware that you're both at least a little fearful. If your partner attacks you, he or she is really requesting love and reassurance.

Rising Above Past-Life Sexual Influences

Understanding the cause is an ideal first step in rising above negative sexual influences. Whether the cause is in the past life or present life, you must go back to the source. Accepting responsibility is your second step towards freedom. Let go of blame and guilt; acknowledge that you karmically set up the experience. Step three is confronting your lesson. Fully explore your emotions and beliefs about the subject. The fourth and final step is honest communication about who you are and what you want. That's when you can begin to *consciously* create your own reality.

PART 2: SEXUAL REPRESSION

Do you feel comfortable making love only in the dark? Would you like your partner to "talk dirty" during sex, but you're too inhibited to ask? Do you find it difficult or impossible to achieve orgasm? Any yes answer amounts to sexual repression.

In our survey of more than 1,000 seminar participants, sexual repression was the most common complaint. The degree of repression varied greatly, from inhibitions about expressing sexual preferences to total rejection of the sex act.

Sally

Sally is divorced, 33, and currently working on her Masters in Business Administration. She states on her questionnaire that she "wants to be more sexually free to moan and groan, rant and rave without reservation." However, she complains of "always being involved with non-communicative men up 'til now."

In regression, Sally re-experienced two lifetimes that strongly related to her verbal repression.

"The first lifetime I recalled took place on the Isle of Man in the 1740s. The sexual climate at that time was quite repressive; sex was considered an obligation to create babies, but on no account was the woman to experience pleasure from it.

"I was married to a man who was very much a product of his time: a deacon in our Calvinist church. He believed that women, like children, should be seen but not heard. Unfortunately, when we bedded I sometimes forgot myself and cried out with pleasure. He responded by slapping me hard, accusing me of being unfaithful and calling me a harlot and slut. This wounded me not just physically, but psychically.

"I guess I must have taken what he said to heart, because in the next lifetime I was a German prostitute. The time was the 1890s. I had a short-lived career. I was not a beauty; the men who took me were rough, the places I worked were rougher. I remember crying during the regression because I was re-experiencing men beating and abusing me. I tried to shut off my feelings, both then and now, to avoid experiencing the pain. When I died at 34, it was not so much from a single beating as the accumulation of too much internal scar tissue.

"This second regression really touched a chord in me. I am very sensitive to touch, but I hate to be touched harshly. I feel a deep panic when someone makes a violent gesture toward me, even if I know they are only play-acting to make a demonstration. I am also very afraid of men who yell, scream or display any kind of violence. This fear of verbal expression from either myself or my partner seems to be a direct connection between my past and present lives. No wonder I choose men who are nonverbal."

My response: In past-life therapy, subjects who are asked to go back to the cause of a particular problem frequently relate experiences that are physically or emotionally traumatic. In each of Sally's past lifetimes, she experienced sex as being painful and humiliating. Today, those experiences manifest in verbal repression. In understanding the cause, and knowing she is no longer in danger, Sally may now be able to risk letting go verbally.

Mark

Mark is a 39-year-old banker who has had three serious relationships, one of them resulting in marriage. "But I have never felt completely connected to any of my lovers," he explains. His primary frustration is a sense of emotional and sexual isolation.

"My first impression of my past life was of being in the womb. I felt so connected, so nurtured, that I didn't want to be born. I recall asking my mother on a superconscious level why we had to be separated, and I felt a great sadness from her. My birth was quite difficult as a result of my resistance, and I believe my mother died during childbirth. I feel guilty now as I think of it.

"My next impression was of being a three-year-old boy. I lived in France; the year was 1798; I was a member of royalty. I was dressed in very stiff, confining clothes. My life, strictly controlled by some kind of guardian, was completely joyless. I was expected to remain dignified at all times, as was fitting for royalty. Slowing I became aware that I was a hemophiliac. That explained the tight control; everyone was constantly worried about me. I remained isolated as I grew up. I believe I was forced to remain celibate, to forego marriage, for fear I might pass on my dread disease. I remained in poor health for a number of years, literally dying for the closeness I had experienced with my mother. At 24 I died, feeling there was absolutely nothing to live for.

"In another regression, I found myself once again swimming in utero. When I asked my Higher Self why I was so attracted to this experience, I received the message that this was one of those rare experiences of being loved unconditionally. I did not have to be anything other than who I was to receive love. I have never experienced this strong sense of connectedness in my waking life. "

My response: Everyone seeks this kind of deep connectedness with another person, yet few experience it. We're afraid if we let go of our defenses and drop our masks, who we are won't be enough to attract or maintain that kind of love. We believe that love, sexual or otherwise, must be deserved.

Most of us, when we fall in love, begin to perform. Making a commitment to a romantic relationship is playing for high stakes. The fear of losing enters your heart. You can no longer afford to be playful, spontaneous, foolish, because being who you are may not measure up to the image you've projected to your new love. The truth is, the person you essentially are is much more magnificent than the mask you're wearing. Masks are caricatures, whereas real people are rich and complex. And infinitely more interesting.

The first step in experiencing a sense of connectedness with someone else is the willingness to expose who you are. People recognize it instantly, and frequently respond by letting down their own defenses. The second step is to totally accept and cherish your lover for everything he or she is, including idiosyncrasies and maddening habits. Not just tolerate, mind you, but accept and cherish. If your lover looks at the world through different eyes, be glad you're now able to see through two pairs, instead of just one. Support your lover in developing his or her own uniqueness. In such an environment, deep, unconditional love—both sexual and otherwise—is born.

Lorna

Lorna is a 34-year-old high school English teacher who has been involved for the last three years in a romantic relationship. On her questionnaire, Lorna stated that she feels she is normally quite sexually open; however, since being with her current lover she has become more and more repressed. Their sexual needs vary widely: she would like to have sex three times a week, he would like it once every three weeks. The goal of her regression was to discover why she was willing to repress herself, or why she was willing to stay in a sexually repressive relationship.

"I found myself in a Gypsy community that had recently moved to a Slavic country. I was sort of royalty: my father had a ridiculously large tent. People paid him money all the time, though he didn't seem to have to work for it. It was a situation I never thought to question.

"As a teenager, I had tawny skin and dark golden hair. I was quite beautiful and owned hundreds of long woven shawls and a pair of silk slippers, which were very rare. I became an incredible flirt. I continually teased and provoked men, especially non-Gypsies in our village. I was particularly heartless with a young dairy farmer who delivered milk. He worked very hard. I would purposely be at the entrance to our tent each day when he appeared with his donkey laden with jugs of milk. I knew he was head over heels in love with me, but I continued to encourage his attentions through my gestures and mannerisms. Once I aroused his ardor, I completely cut off my communication with him. In his despair, he committed suicide.

"That young man of my regressive experience is definitely my present-day boyfriend. I sense that his past-life anger and bitterness, his sense of inadequacy, is affecting our relationship today. Perhaps I have repressed that part of myself due to my feelings of guilt over my treatment of him during that life. Clearly, we both must forgive each other for our terrible past before we can be free of its influences."

My response: One interpretation of Lorna's past and present-life experiences would be simple karma: her boyfriend today is punishing her for negative past behavior.

However, a more meaningful interpretation can be made if

you look at karma as cause-and-effect. In Lorna's case, the past-life cause is sexual enticement and rejection. The present-day effect is sexual repression to avoid rejection.

You can't have sex and not have sex at the same time, but that is what many couples try to do. They want to be naked without being vulnerable, and the result is sexual repression. But sexual repression does not protect you from being hurt. All it does is dull the senses to both pain and pleasure.

Lorna has nothing to lose by risking sexual openness with her boyfriend. At best, it gives him the opportunity to respond differently to her. At worst, she discovers he is unwilling to take the same risk and that leaves her free to choose from a position of knowledge.

Eva

Eva is a 34-year-old television news researcher. She has recently become involved with a 43-year-old man whom she describes as "very successful, worldly but innocent." Her primary sexual issue is repression and inability to achieve orgasms. Her regression explains why.

"Phillip, my current boyfriend, and I were involved together in an early Christian community. I don't believe we were physical lovers, for it felt as if we were very pure and innocent. I was headed for the convent; Philip for the priesthood. Our Christian ideals were so sincerely shared, our spirituality so important, that we were above physical lust.

"Today, I believe that Philip and I are back together to resume the purity of love and trust and Christian values we once shared. Although Philip has subscribed to materialistic values in his life, he is now going through a mid-life evaluation. I'm the first woman to introduce him to a new experience of himself. I feel that I am here to support his turning to spiritual values once again."

My response: With the set of beliefs that Eva cherishes, there is no way for her to allow herself to enjoy sex, much less achieve orgasm. She believes spirituality excludes sexuality, and since she's chosen a "spiritual" path, she must now be "above physical lust."

If your sexual reality isn't working for you, the best place to seek an answer is in your own mind. In addition to doing the sexual beliefs process in chapter nine, write down all the beliefs you have about sex.

If, in your search you discover old, useless beliefs that inhibit you sexually, write them on a separate list. When you feel you've exhausted every feeling, thought or belief you have about sex, take a look at the list of beliefs that don't work. Create a positive affirmation that programs the beliefs you'd like to transplant. For example, if you believe that wanting sex isn't spiritual, a new affirmation might be: "I am a spiritual being experiencing life in a physical body. I value all the experiences available to me as a physical being, including my sexuality."

If you believe that being completely uninhibited about sex will leave you open to hurt and rejection, you might create this affirmation: "I am a highly desirable person who is completely open about sex. My partners are delighted by my openness and respond warmly to me."

In creating your affirmations, make sure they are phrased positively, in the present tense as an already accomplished fact. Then repeat the affirmations in an altered state of consciousness to magnify their power. As the power of your new beliefs are magnified, so is the power you have over your sexual experiences.

PART 3: PROBLEMS, PREFERENCES & PRACTICES

Carla

Carla is a 32-year-old housewife and mother, married to her second husband for five years; they have a two-year-old son. Carla is frigid.

When asked to go back to the cause of her current sexual issue, Carla had the following experience:

"I found myself in a remote English country home. There were huge dark mountains surrounding the house, which cut off the sunlight in the middle of the day. I was married to a staid but gentle older man named Tudor. I, on the other hand, was still young and frivolous. I longed for the excitement of my former life in London, and I deeply resented being exiled in this dark, ugly place.

"One day my cousin Eddie came to visit. He brought a friend with him, a man named Nettles. They stayed for quite some time, playing croquet, going on picnics and so on. It was wonderful to have an audience again.

"I fell head over heels in love with Nettles. Or rather, I fell head over heels in love with the notion of escape he offered. True to the unspoken traditions of the day, I made love with him to bind him to me through guilt. We made our plans to run away together.

"I am shocked, now, at how shallow and callous I was then. I childishly blamed my loving husband for the lack of excitement in my life. I remember thinking, 'It serves him right for me to leave ... locking me up in this dreary old dungeon.'

"One afternoon when Tudor was away, Nettles and I stayed in bed. He entertained me with stories about the life we would lead together.

"Tudor walked in, his grim face revealing that he had known far more than I suspected of my betrayal. He had a gun in his hand. Without a word, he shot Nettles in the chest. Thinking I was next, I ran to Tudor and, dropping to press myself against his knees, I begged for mercy.

"He yanked me up to stand in front of him. 'Shut up!" he cried. 'Your death will not be nearly so quick and painless as his. Instead, you'll be forced to stay in this dungeon, as you call it, for the rest of your days. No visitors will be admitted. You may not leave. If I catch you in the attempt, I will kill you.'

"With that, he left my bedroom, locking the door from the outside. Servants came up later to remove Nettle's body, but I was left alone for days to weep and rave about the horrors I was enduring. Out of this terrible pain I chose to spend the rest of my life hating Tudor. I was not wise enough to realize I had created the whole experience. It was much easier to blame him.

"And that is precisely what I am doing today. I am married once again to Tudor. Though I no longer hate him consciously, when we have sex, I experience the most unbelievable feelings of resentment. And since I wasn't frigid before becoming involved with him, I've also blamed him for my frigidity.

"Now I realize that I've set the whole thing up as a learning experience. I need to grow beyond hate and guilt, and accept the fact that I am responsible for all I experience.

"What a mind-blowing session!"

My response: Because the strong emotions Carla experienced in her past life were incomplete and unresolved, she was forced to repeat them. To discover your past-life sexual influences, look for the aspects of your sexuality that create strong emotions. Fear, pain, rage, or guilt from a past life may manifest as tension, inhibitions or anxieties in this life. The key is to look for those emotions that cannot be adequately explained by current life experiences and programming. Once you've identified the emotion, use regressive hypnosis to go back to the cause.

Nancy

Nancy is a 35-year-old woman who feels that sexual desire is something to rise above in pursuit of spirituality. She believes her current attitudes about sex were formed during her lifetime as a priestess in ancient Egypt.

"As soon as I stepped out the tunnel, I knew I was in the right lifetime. I couldn't see anything yet, but the emotions I felt—an almost euphoric calm—are emotions I've wanted to experience throughout this life. I've had a taste of it, but never the intensity of what I felt during this session.

"Dick had instructed us to just follow our emotions and see where they led us. When I focused on my feelings, the blackness around me began to dissolve.

"I found myself walking up stairs leading to a temple. I was studying to become a priestess. I walked into a class being held in a formal room with a high, domed ceiling. There were several other girls there, as well as an instructress.

"All of the girls were in their early teens. We were from wealthy, aristocratic families. Everyone knew that being a priestess was the greatest honor one could achieve.

"The instructress was explaining about our role as women, as compared to the roles of most women. She told us we were special, different. That we would never marry or have children, but instead would have an intimate relationship with God. She explained that becoming physically involved with men would prevent us from being a clear channel for God.

"I remember feeling, 'But of course.' We had all been groomed for our roles from our earliest memories. Because of this, I think we all felt a mild contempt for 'ordinary' women. Certainly, we did not want to be like them.

"I stayed in that classroom for the entire hypnotic regression. It was the most peaceful, fulfilling experience I have ever had. I only wish I would have stayed permanently."

My response: Nancy's viewpoint was appropriate for her Egyptian lifetime, but according to her questionnaire, it doesn't translate well into this incarnation. Many others who have experienced spiritually enlightening lifetimes in past-life regression have experienced the same conflict.

If rising above sexual desire works in your life, that's fine. However, you have chosen this lifetime to learn new lessons and have new experiences. You have chosen a physical form for its unique opportunities.

CHAPTER 8

HOMOSEXUAL & BISEXUAL INFLUENCES FROM PAST LIVES

Research Project Continued

In my work with thousands of seminar participants on the sexual influence of past lives, I've never heard the same experience twice. Each person had a unique set of memories that were affecting them today. These memories fell primarily into one of three patterns: 1) The carryover of strong emotions from a traumatic past-life experience; 2) Current preferences/practices related to socially-acceptable sexual morals of a significant previous life; 3) A karmic lifestyle choice to provide growth opportunities, but not necessarily directly relating to a sexual situation from previous incarnations.

The focus of this segment is bisexuality and homosexuality. From a spiritual perspective, the decision to be gay, bi or straight is a karmic lifestyle choice. We choose, before being born, the sexual preference that offers us the greatest opportunity for growth.

As with the previous chapter, these cases were part of a series that originally ran in *Reincarnation Report* magazine.

Ray

"My first impression was of myself walking into a study with a group of men. We were retiring for the traditional cigars and brandy after a full meal. The talk was all of Lincoln's foolhardy notion about freeing the slaves. None of us could take it seriously. We thought of blacks as domesticated animals dependent on white masters for food and shelter. None of us were cruel to our slaves; we prided ourselves on our 'humanitarian' treatment. We thought, smugly, that we knew, far better than Lincoln, what was best for blacks.

"My next impression was of a flurry of excitement. War had been declared. We were going to show those Yankees that one Southern gentleman was as good as any two Yankees. We were like little boys delighted to have a new game to play.

"I didn't see this, but I somehow knew that I was killed early in the war. I know for sure that I died believing that we were right. That blacks had their place, just like women and children, and it sure wasn't on an equal level with men.

"Looking back on the experience, I can't believe the self-righteousness of my attitude. God, to feel that sure you have all the answers. It's something I've fought against all my life.

"Come to think of it, I seem to have set up my experiences to be the exact opposite of the previous lifetime. As a homosexual, I am definitely outside the mainstream of society. That doesn't make me angry, but it does bring me into direct contact with other people's self-righteous attitudes. It also allows me to be empathetic to the trials of other minorities, including blacks. Knowing this makes me really glad I chose to be gay."

Belinda

Belinda is a 38-year-old phone company installer, who lives with Sherry, her girlfriend of two years. In the back-to-the-cause regression, Belinda explored why she always assumes the dominant role in her relationships.

"I love being with women, but I'm not sure I love being a woman. For as long as I can remember, I have always assumed a 'male' role in my relationships, even to the point of financially supporting my girlfriends. I don't want to perpetuate that kind of unbalanced relationship.

"This was my first experience with hypnosis. At first, I received some confusing images ... as if I were seeing one life after another, all in rapid succession. In each of the lifetimes, I saw myself as a man. I can't describe how relieved and satisfied I felt. It's as if I felt complete for the first time in my life.

"Finally, my mind consented to focus on one lifetime. I found myself in Boston in the 1920s. Once again I was a man. In this lifetime, I was married to a pretty young woman; we had a small child. I re-experienced my pleasure in coming home from my bank each evening to find dinner ready, the fire lit, my child already dressed in his bedclothes. It was utter harmony.

"As our son grew up and went off to school, my wife was left with time on her hands. She grew bored, and in her restlessness she became interested in the women's suffragette movement. Her interest quickly became all-consuming passion. Night after night, all I heard about were women's issues: women's right to vote, to work, etc. Our home was littered with leaflets, meals were never ready on time. My sense of harmony was completely shattered.

"I hated this movement for taking my wife from me. In fact, I began to hate all women, thinking them ungrateful and willful. I decided to put my foot down. I told my wife that if she did not abandon her interest in the suffragettes, she would be forced to abandon our home. After many tearful arguments she submitted. She was not yet ready to imagine supporting herself financially, and in any case, the mores of our time were contemptuous of single or divorced women. We negotiated an uneasy truce, but never returned to the happy comfort of our former life. I think we both harbored a secret grudge for the rest of our days."

My response: Belinda has experienced several male lifetimes, which probably explains why she so easily relates to the male viewpoint. Unconsciously, she also remembers the harmony of life with a subservient woman, an experience she may be attempting to recreate in her current life. Since Belinda and her previous wife never resolved their feelings about their roles, Belinda is still attempting to sort it out.

From another perspective, in her past life, Belinda repressed her wife by denying her the opportunity to follow her own passionate interests. Today, Belinda has given herself a chance to learn this lesson in two ways: first, by experiencing what life is like when you're denied opportunities as a woman; and second, by becoming romantically involved with women and choosing whether or not to dominate them. Viewed in this light, it's easy to see why being a gay woman was an appropriate lifestyle choice.

Phillip

Phillip is a 29-year-old divorce lawyer. He has been gay since his initiation at 15, but rarely maintains a relationship more than six months. In hypnotic regression, Phillip searched for the cause of his depressing sense of isolation.

"I have always had trouble relating emotionally to any of my partners. I am sexually attracted to men, but I feel a strong need to separate my sexual self from my career self or even human self. This dilemma prevents me from experiencing any warmth or satisfaction in my life. I'd really like to know why.

"In the regression, as soon as I was standing outside the time tunnel, I had a clear picture of myself. I was a man dressed in monk's robes, sitting quietly in an abbey. There were many other men around me who seemed to be praying.

"I was not praying. I was mentally reliving the previous night. It had been a euphoric day. After five years of diligent effort, I had finally completed copying one of the sacred books. I took the copy to celebrate with my dearest friend, a fellow monk. When I entered his room I could hardly contain my excitement. He stood up to congratulate me. We embraced. And then ... we didn't let go. We held each other for the longest time, silently expressing the love we had shared for many years.

"With a single gesture, he led me to his bed. We stayed there for many hours, reveling in the joy of saying what we had always suppressed, expressing what we had always withheld. It was the most powerful emotional experience of that lifetime ... or this.

"Late that night, I returned to my room. For hours I lay, sleepless with joy and satisfaction. This euphoria lasted only till sunrise. Somehow with the return of daylight came also the full weight of the values I had lived by all those years. The contempt for any form of sexuality. The admiration of every form of self-discipline.We had violated a taboo not even permissible to commoners, much less to monks.

"When I saw my friend next, my heart tightened into a knot of self-contempt. I faced him coldly, determined to pretend the previous night had not existed. He understood at once. And in that moment, we ended our friendship forever."

My response: Unresolved emotions are among the most powerful past-life influences. Subconsciously, Phillip relates love to self-destruction. By being courageous enough to give and receive love, he may be able to rise above this false-guilt karma.

Dora

Dora is a 24-year-old hairdresser. She has been involved in love-hate relationships with women since her early teens. Although her sexual preference has always been for women, she has hidden that fact behind a series of casual relationships with men. Her primary sexual issue is her conflicting attraction and opposition to being gay.

"I don't like to think of myself as gay. I mean, it doesn't seem normal. So I try to date men, but I always end up in bed with one of my girlfriends. I guess what I most want to find out about is why I feel compelled to be with women, when being gay causes me to feel like a social outcast.

"When we were told in the regression to begin to perceive our surroundings, all I saw was blackness. I couldn't see my shoes, or my clothes, or anything. But boy, my feelings went crazy. I got goosebumps all over. My stomach tightened into a hard knot. My heart was pounding. All I could feel was hatred and disgust. It almost made me open my eyes.

"But Dick had told us to just trust the experience and our impressions, so I tried to explore how I felt. 'Where did all this hatred come from?' I asked myself. That's when I began to see pictures.

"The first thing I saw was my feet. I was wearing some dark, hard shoes, laced up tight. My legs were covered by wide black skirts; I could feel the bodice tight against my rather wide waist. I realized that I was a Quaker.

"As I began to view the scene with my mind's eyes—it's funny how selective that vision is—I perceived that I was standing in a large group of people gathered at the town square. I sensed that the rest of the crowd felt just as hostile, just as hateful, as I did. I began to search for the reason.

"On the platform in front of me stood a woman. Her head was bowed, and my heart went out to her as I felt her shame. That is, the me that I am now felt empathetic. The me that I was then felt some sort of ugly, dark pleasure.

"It was obvious that the woman was pregnant. As I watched, a solemn-looking man stepped up on the platform. He had a megaphone of some kind in his hand. Without looking at the woman, he began to read from a scroll of papers. 'Katherine Brandon has been accused of committing adultery with Nathaniel Duncan, husband of Elizabeth Duncan and father of Nathaniel, Jr., James and Dorothy. She bears his illegitimate child. By the laws of this Christian community, we cannot permit any among us to live in flagrant violation of the Holy Writ. Is there any man here who will take her for his wife and give her child a name?'

"Several moments of gut-wrenching silence passed while the townspeople furtively glanced everywhere but at the speaker.

The tension was almost suffocating.

"At last, the speaker cleared his throat as he said, 'Then she cannot continue to live among us. We will make arrangements for her passage into the woods, where she will have to make her own way ...'

"I was horror-stricken. I knew they were pronouncing her death sentence. Suddenly, a woman's voice roared, 'Stone the filthy tramp, I say.' It was my voice, or rather, the voice of the woman I was in this past life. I burst into tears as I felt her reach down and pick up a large stone. She heaved it at the woman on the platform ...

"At once, I was wide awake. Shaking and trembling. Filled with self-hatred. How could I ever have been so mean, so spiteful, so sure of moral righteousness. How I wished to make it up to the woman I had wronged so long ago.

"And then it dawned on me. That's exactly what I'm doing. Today, I live on the outside of socially acceptable sexual preferences. I'm experiencing, in my own way, what that poor woman endured in another century."

My response: Dora needs to learn tolerance and compassion for those who have different values. Knowing the reason for her lifestyle choice, and desiring spiritual growth, she will now recognize growth opportunities (tests) as they arise. How she handles these situations will dictate her progress.

Ben

Ben is a 45-year-old commercial photographer. He's long been divorced from his marriage of 10 years, although he and his ex-wife remain close. Ben considers himself bisexual, and proud of it. His motive for exploring past lives was curiosity.

"I've often wondered how I managed to escape the programming of my generation. I grew up surrounded by traditional values of family and fidelity, yet I never bought their ideas about the horrors of homosexuality. I had my first homosexual affair when I was 20, and I've shared myself with both men and women ever since. Where did I get such a relaxed attitude about sexual preferences?

"My first regressive impression was of myself running along a beach with a group of boys. We were all about 15, and dressed in short togas. I had a sense of being in ancient Greece.

"After the run we returned to the gymnasium, where we all jumped into a collective bath. We were laughing and splashing water. Some of the boys toweled each other off and walked away, arms around each other's shoulders. No one reacted in any way; it was obviously considered socially acceptable.

"My next impression was of walking through crowded city streets. There was a fair going on, and many vendors were selling their wares on street corners. Men and women were dancing with each other as well as with members of their own sex. I was excited to see a woman I admired dancing with a close friend of mine. Without a second thought, I joined their dance. They laughed and welcomed me. We joined hands and began dancing in a circle. Then the woman released my friend's hand and began to wind us, snake fashion through the crowds. We ended up in the doorway of the house she shared with her parents. With nothing but a smile, the three of us stepped into her room and tumbled onto her bed. We made love together till dusk.

"My first reaction after coming back from the regression was: 'This is too good to be true.' I wondered if I had just made up the whole experience to justify my freedom-loving sexual preferences. Yet I'd have to say that the emotional quality of the experience really hit home with me. As uninhibited as I like to imagine myself, nothing in this life compares to the innocence and pure happiness I experienced in this regression. Perhaps I started out that whole, but lost some of myself to the restrictive programming of my youth. All I know is, I'm now going to work to recapture that essence in my life today."

My response: "Recapturing your essence" is another way of expressing your earthly purpose. We deliberately set up lessons that will allow us to grow beyond our fearful beliefs—some of which relate to our sexuality. Our sexual preference brings us face-to-face with these beliefs, and provides ongoing opportunities to express unconditional love.

"Controversial Questions"
Column In "Master of Life Winners"

Q.

When you offered the "Strong Immune System" hypnosis tape free to anyone who has tested HIV positive, it seemed to me that you were endorsing homosexuality—which is as far from spirituality as you can get.

A.

Since you know so much about spirituality, you're familiar with this Universal Law: "That which you resist, you draw to you." And if you don't learn by contact, another law goes into effect: "That which you resist you become." Since you obviously fear homosexuality, if you don't resolve it, you could probably reincarnate as a lesbian. First-hand experience will help you integrate your fear.

Q.

Recent medical findings indicate that homosexuality is genetically determined. How does this align with your idea that to be gay is a karmic lifestyle choice?

A.

Perfectly. Prior to birth, you choose parents (a genetic lineage), circumstances (country, rural/city location, monetary conditions, et cetera) and a birth time that will set you on a karmic path. One soul picks artistic parents to assure an artistic path. Another chooses to be Swedish. Someone else, artistic, Swedish

125

and gay. We each have things we desire to learn. Maybe we can learn them faster as gay, straight, bi, black, white, yellow, American, Hispanic, or Chinese people.

Learning opportunities are always changing. A gay friend told me he had explored past-life regression to find out why he was HIV positive today. "I was once a womanizing playboy with syphilis. I knew I had the disease, but that didn't stop me from having unprotected sex with every woman I could seduce."

"Does understanding the cause help you accept?" I asked.

"Knowing that I'm resolving karma helps. It also helps to know that it has nothing to do with being gay. But if wisdom erases karma, I'm going to beat AIDS with an ultra-healthy lifestyle and positive programming."

I should add that in his new profession, he helps others with the disease.

Another gay man explained, "In regression, I saw myself as a redneck who hated homosexuals."

A lesbian woman told me, "I chose to reincarnate gay to be with Carla again. We're soulmates and this is a relationship aspect we had not experienced."

"Can you explain more?" I asked.

"We've often been together in male/female roles, and we were always distracted by children and responsibilities. This life is a reward. We both have well-paying jobs, so life isn't a struggle, and we get to focus all our attention upon each other."

Q.

Some gay publications say you are either straight or gay, there is no such thing as bisexuality? Since you openly write on this subject and also view such earthly concerns from a spiritual perspective, I'd like your opinion.

A.

My research indicates those who claim to be bi are capable

of fully enjoying sex with both males and females. Bhagwan Shree Rajneesh says, "Basically a bisexual person is more rich sexually than the heterosexual or the homosexual, because he has two dimensions in him. There is every possibility that the future is going to be more bisexual than homo or hetero because bisexuality means that two dimensions are possible."

Respected researcher Jamake Highwater in his book *Myth & Sexuality,* says, "... if we want to understand the way in which the Greeks themselves understood this ambiguity of desire, we must take into account the fact that they did not recognize two different drives. When we speak of their 'bisexuality' we are probably thinking that they allowed themselves a choice between the sexes, whereas, for them, this option was not an expression of a dual, ambivalent, and bisexual desire. As Foucault puts it, 'To their way of thinking, what made it possible to desire a man or a woman was simply the appetite that nature had implanted in man's heart for beautiful human beings, whatever their sex might be.'"

CHAPTER 9

SETTING SEX AND RELATIONSHIPS FREE

"Nearly half of the people who read my magazine and attend my seminars are single; many are looking for and not finding the right mate. Others are unhappily married. Then consider the divorce rate and the number of single parents. Relationships and family units are destined to take many different forms as we move into the next century."
—Seminar dialogue

Your best "mirrors" for learning to respond to life harmoniously are your relationships with family, friends, in-laws, co-workers ... and especially your lovers, because sex always generates complex issues and emotional peaks and valleys to test your awareness. The opportunities are endless—from fear-based emotions, such as insecurity and petty expectations, to potentials such as trust and commitment.

* * * * *

"I want a twin-flame soulmate relationship!"

I've heard this a thousand times in seminars, and I've read it over and over in letters. "I want a warm, loving, sexually satisfying, one-on-one relationship that allows us both to grow and evolve," they say. And judging by the number of people expressing this goal, it is the ideal of metaphysically oriented people. The problem is, only a tiny percentage of the population experiences such a relationship.

"Those who find their soulmates are being karmically rewarded," I'm told. "They're lucky!"

Maybe. But there is one factor common to people sharing soulmate relationships: *they tend to be self-actualized.* Maybe, because of their awareness, they are manifesting more successful relationships.

My research shows that lovers are all experiencing a predestined soulmate relationship: "Karmic Companions" are two people destined to form a union to confront unlearned lessons from past lives. "Dharmic-Bond Soulmates" share a goal. "Twin-flame (or counterpart) soulmates" have ideal relationships and are together to work on other things.

To experience the twin-flame ideal, maybe you have to view life from a more self-actualized perspective. It seems to be so.

Wisdom erases karma, so yes, twin-flame soulmates are experiencing a karmic reward—self-bestowed as the result of expanded awareness. Maybe they started out as karmic companions, or dharmic-bond soulmates, and went on to become more.

I've already written several books about one-on-one relationships. Having established that I have not ignored the "straight and normal," I intend to focus upon some radical relationship and sexual ideas.

Whose Model?

The Religious Right wants us to look backward for a relationship model—a "traditional value" Ozzie and Harriet lifestyle that never existed. But these ultra-conservatives don't want us to look too far back in history, because we'll find many models in our Pagan roots that are not acceptable today. But why aren't they acceptable? From a nonjudgmental, spiritual perspective, if no one is harmed, how can any combination of people sharing life and love be wrong? For those who aren't finding a "standard" relationship, why not consider alternatives? For those who are not comfortable with society's model, why not explore potentials that were once commonly accepted and which I believe will be again sometime in the near future?

Alternative lifestyles threaten church and state, because they are "freeing." This means they have the potential to become generally accepted. Given a choice between equally acceptable alternatives, people will usually choose freedom. So the church/state must eliminate the counter-culture alternatives or make them unacceptable in the eyes of society. Free people can't be made to feel guilty and tithe, so the church/state loses control, which translates as loss of income that threatens the survival of the religious institution.

If you have any doubt that church and state are in bed together, look at the current political climate. The Religious Right has helped elect politicians to protect its interests and pass laws to enforce its tenets.

"Controversial Questions"

Q.

Why don't you believe our spiritual goal is to repress sexuality and evolve to celibacy?

A.

Celibacy is demanded by most cults, and encouraged by many religions, so you think it is spiritual. These organizations know that sex is such a powerful force, it can not be successfully repressed. When followers fail to contain their sexuality, they feel guilty, which is just what the guru/priest wants. It is easier to control guilty people. When the followers continue to fail, they lose self-esteem. They accept that they are sinners and the guru or church becomes their only hope of redemption. A very successful ploy.

You incarnated to let go of fear and raise your level of awareness by interacting harmoniously with physical reality. When you reject an aspect of physical reality (sex), you are not living life fully. Until you can live a life of total involvement, without experiencing fearful attachments, you'll continue to be tied to the earth.

Repression is a fearful attachment we all experience. The problem with repression is it never goes away. It will always surface when you grow tired of resisting it. So, from the perspective of generating disharmonious karma, repression is worse than indulgence (as long as you are not harming anyone else through your indulgence), because you eventually get tired of what you indulge in.

Bhagwan Shree Rajneesh was considered the "sex guru"—a teacher bold enough to go against the spiritual grain and encourage people to explore their sexuality (it was also great marketing). He felt his followers would move past their sexual obsessions faster through indulgence rather than through repression. Then they would be free to concentrate upon spirituality.

The Pagan side of esoteric metaphysics teaches that to repress who you really are generates a vibrational energy that will have to be expressed—if not in this life, in the next. When sexual energy is repressed, it becomes perverted or turns to anger, which is why armies have historically used forced abstinence to channel anger onto the battlefield.

Q.

I despised your answer (above). The idea isn't to repress your sexual drive. The idea is to transmute sexuality into a higher pursuit.

A.

Without repression, unless you're naturally asexual, it's about as likely to happen as transmuting lead into gold.

Q.

Obviously, from the permissive sexual attitudes reflected in your writings, you don't see homosexuality or sexual transgressions as sins. I'm curious. Do you see anything as sinful?

A.

The root meaning of the word "sin" is to miss the mark. That takes a little of the hellfire out of the concept, doesn't it? I think you're missing the mark if you purposely hurt other human beings, mentally or physically. I think you miss the mark when you sell or trade aliveness for survival. And I think you miss the mark when you manipulate someone for selfish purposes.

In regard to homosexuality, I agree with actor Paul Newman, who says, "I'm a supporter of gay rights. And not a closet supporter, either. From the time I was a kid, I have never been able to understand attacks on the gay community. There are so many qualities that make up a human being ... by the time I get through with all the things that I really admire about people, what they do with their private parts is probably so low on the list that it is irrelevant."

Bushido Training
Sex Talk & Belief Process

Concepts of morality have swung like a pendulum back and forth through history. In twelfth century England, to think of sex was considered a sin, even if you were married. The "missionary" position was the only acceptable coital position, and only for the purpose of begetting children. Sex was totally forbidden on Sundays, Wednesdays, Fridays and for forty days before Christmas or Easter. Any pleasure experienced from this regrettably necessary act of perpetuating the race was also considered a sin.

Between A.D. 800 and A.D. 1000 in England, people experienced a much freer sexual morality. Celibacy was considered unhealthy, and extensive prostitution was supported by authorities. Public nudity was accepted at beaches and women were free to take lovers regardless of their marital status. Men were free to seduce women of lower rank and could seek the favors of women of equal or higher rank according to the customs of the day.

The Inquisition was really a move by the Christian Church to eliminate a competitive and sexually-open religion—Paganism.

In ancient Sparta the public nudity of both young men and women was encouraged. Young people experienced considerable sexual freedom before marriage, as celibacy was considered a crime. It was acceptable for older men to "loan" their wives to relatives or friends for the purpose of bearing a child if the combination might result in a superior human specimen.

In Greece, homosexuality was commonly accepted, and many regarded the love between two men to be the highest form of love. Grecian women received little education, with the exception of courtesans who were well educated to better serve as companions for the men. Courtesans had more freedom than any group of women in Greek society and were often very wealthy. There was no stigma attached to their profession and they were received in the highest circles.

Is it surprising that we have the sexual confusion and problems that exist today? We are old souls who have lived many lives that have programmed us with conflicting ideas of morality. As the sum total of all our previous experiences, we have innate feelings about what is right and wrong for us. Depending upon your past programming, your current sexual orientation may or may not be compatible with our current society's mores.

If sex is not the most important issue in your life, it is one of the top two or three. Problems come from repression in this area. You worry that maybe you're weird. You wonder if you're the only one that thinks this, or does that. And this lowers self-esteem and makes sex an issue.

To show you just how predictable we all are, I've gathered some sexual facts from six highly-respected research studies—all published in book form. Where percentages are provided, I've averaged the percentages from all the studies.

- 82 percent of women masturbate (have or do).
- 83 percent of men masturbate on a regular basis, married or not. 8 percent several times a day. 9 percent daily. 28 percent several times a week. 22 percent once every two weeks.
- At least 20 percent of all women have had a homosexual experience to orgasm.
- One third of all men have had a homosexual experience to orgasm.
- Statistics indicate much higher percentages of people who would like to have a homosexual experience but do not out of fear or lack of opportunity.
- It is believed by many sexual researchers from Freud and Kinsey and more recently psychiatrist Dr. Charlotte Wolfe, that each of us is inherently bisexual. It is only our social mores that keep us from expressing who we are.
- Over one third of all married women have had an affair. And only a small percentage of these were because of deep emotional dissatisfaction with their husband.
- Over one half of all married men have had an affair.
- One percent of women have been sexually involved with an animal. In a city of one million, that's 10,000 women.
- One out of seven women have been raped.

Now, from the researcher's reports, let's look at some of women's top ten sexual fantasies: Sex with a man she has not previously been involved with. Group sex. Sex with more than one man at the same time.

From the list of men's top ten fantasies: Sex with a woman he has not previously been involved with. Sex with two or more women at the same time. His wife or lover having sex with another man.

These are just some current facts about what is with sex. You're not abnormal. And you're not abnormal if none of these statistics or fantasies relate to you. It's time to stop judging yourself and others. There is no such thing as right or wrong, moral or immoral. There is only what we *call* moral and immoral at this moment in time. If the church or society agrees to call a particular practice immoral, that doesn't make it so.

It is time to get off of your sexual stuckness and integrate any sexual repression you're experiencing. Then it's time to ask yourself, "Does what I do sexually work for me? Does it manifest love, health, happiness, aliveness and allow me full self-expression?"

Bushido Seminar
Sex Beliefs Process

This is a process to explore your sexual beliefs, and to uncover any repressed beliefs that are not serving you. In the seminar training this group process is conducted in an altered state of consciousness, but it can be quite effective for a reader to mentally finish the following incomplete sentences. **How you respond will expose your deep-seated beliefs.** Read and respond instantly, the way you really feel. Do not consider how you "should" feel. Note if your response is positive or negative, and mentally flag those sentences that generate an emotional response.

Sex is ...

Sex should be ...

When it comes to openly and honestly communicating my sexual desires to my partner, I ...

Discussing sex makes me feel ...

When I think about my sexual limitations, I ...

When I masturbate, I feel ...

If my primary sexual partner were to rate me as a lover on a scale of one to ten, I'd probably get a ...

My heterosexual thoughts and fantasies make me feel ...

My homosexual thoughts and fantasies make me feel ...

When I think about what I do sexually, I feel ...

When I think about my sexual past, I feel ...

Someone said that other people, the church and society inflict their sexual beliefs on you, and you accept them. I think the person who said this is ...

NOTE: The next sentences refer to sexual practices that are not necessarily approved of by society. Some people enhance their lives with exhibitionism, bondage, consensual non-monogamy, group sex, polyfidelity, or other forms of sexual adventure.

When I think of participating in this kind of sexual activity, I feel ...

When I think about allowing my mate or lover to participate in this kind of sexual adventure, I feel ...

The thought of my mate or lover having an affair makes me feel ...

When I think about experiencing gay sex, I feel ...

When I think about experiencing heterosexual intercourse, I feel ...

The idea of my mate or lover having gay sex makes me feel ...

The idea of my mate or lover having heterosexual intercourse makes me feel ...

If I could do anything I wanted sexually, without worrying about what anyone else thought, I would like to ...

If I were to measure the level of my sexual openness on a scale of one to ten, I'd have to rate myself as a ...

If I were to compare how open I am sexually to the quality of my sex life, I would have to conclude ...

* * * * *

Some participating in this process don't get enough sex. Others get more than they want. Some are frustrated because of unfulfilled desires. Some are feeling guilty about what they do

137

sexually, or what they've done in the past. Some are afraid to do what they really want to do. Some are shocked by their desires. Some feel unnecessarily guilty. Some need to find love. Some can't reconcile spirituality with sexuality.

Whatever your situation, it can be traced back to your beliefs ... beliefs that were programmed as the result of past experiences. Even if an improvement in your sex life depends upon someone else changing, it is your karma or you wouldn't find yourself in the situation. In other words, there is a karmic-belief block that you've set into motion for the learning opportunity it provides. Sometimes these blocks are to balance past deeds, and sometimes they reflect false guilt or false-fear karma that is easily overcome once it is recognized.

NOTE: In the seminar training the participants are hypnotically regressed at this point: "In just a moment you're going to regress back to your past in this life, or a past life, to find the cause of the sexual situation you'd most like to explore. If you have deep-seated beliefs about sexuality that are working against you, what are they? Consider the primary belief that may not be serving you, and in just a moment I'll regress you back to the situation that set it into effect."

* * * * *

Following the hypnotic regression, I ask the participants to share what they experienced in the process and to ask questions. Those desiring to release repressed fears by sharing their sexual secrets are invited to do so. This is always a cathartic experience for everyone in the seminar room.

Follow-up Dialogues
1.

"I have great sex with my husband, but when I masturbate, I always fantasize about doing it with a big black man. I don't even know any black men, so it's kind of strange why this turns me on the way it does," Mary said, stroking her fingers through her long blonde hair. She was in her late twenties or early thirties and dressed like she'd just stepped out of the pages of *Elle* magazine.

"What was the cause?" I asked.

"I was a black woman, married to a big black man in San Francisco around the turn of the century, I think. We lived in a little apartment over a store. My most vivid impression was of him coming home and me waiting in bed. He was dressed fancy, like he worked some place that required him to dress up. I just laid there watching him undress while he stared into my eyes ... smiling. Wow!"

2.

"When I start to have an orgasm, I panic," said Beth, a demure-looking woman in her forties. "I'd like to be able to scream with joy, but instead, I bite my tongue to keep from expressing anything. My husband doesn't even know when ..." She smiled shyly, looked at the floor.

"You're in a safe environment to discuss it, Beth. Maybe it will help to integrate the fear."

She nodded and said, "In regression, I only saw one scene, but it was very vivid. I was a male with long black hair, and I was sneaking into a tiny room illuminated by something burning in a dish of tallow. The walls were plastered in mud and my lover lay on a bed of animal skins. She welcomed me with open arms, and we immediately began to make love. I think we made too much noise, because men came rushing into the room, grabbed me and dragged me outside. Naked, they tied me to a tree, and the girl's father lit a torch. They made her watch. When she screamed, one of the men held his hand over her mouth. Her father placed the burning torch beneath my genitals."

Beth's voice quivered. "As you instructed, there was no pain, but my emotional reaction, I counted myself up out of hypnosis."

"False-fear karma, Beth. Your subconscious mind is programmed to believe if you make noise during sex, you'll be punished. Explain this to your husband, and then confront the fear by making loud passionate love. Once your subconscious realizes you won't be punished, it will probably get over it."

"But this seemed to be in ancient times. I've had other regressions, and I know I've lived many lifetimes between then and now. Why would I have to have waited so long to confront this?"

"Karma doesn't necessarily unfold in sequential time. Each incarnation offers an opportunity to best confront particular programming. Sometimes you wait until all the key players can reunite. And I've seen effects like this that carried over from lifetime to lifetime. You may not have openly expressed during sex for many incarnations. Cause and effect works in many ways. As an example, in a following male incarnation, the fearful punishment could have resulted in impotence."

Beth nodded. "The father in that past life could be someone in my present life?"

"Maybe? You could find out in hypnosis."

"It probably explains the relationship between my husband and my step-father."

3.

"I'm gay and I have a lot of lovers. After that process, I don't feel so guilty about it," said Scott, a casually dressed young man.

"Some people use concepts such as freedom and openness as rationals for failure to relate wholly to anyone else. If that's what you're doing, Scott, it isn't working."

"Oh," he said, sitting down.

4.

"My marriage is a *menage a trois*," said Jonathan, a well-dressed man I guessed to be in his mid-forties. "For eleven years, I've lived with a woman and another man. David and I are bisexual, Debbie is straight. So we each have two lovers. It's always seemed so natural."

"Is it a good marriage?" I asked.

Jonathan laughed. "I don't know how it could be better. We all love and support each other. Two male incomes give us plenty of money. Debbie stays home with the children. She had one child by David and one by me. The only external problems our marriage has created are with the teachers at the children's school. Of course, the IRS refuses to recognize our union." He paused. "Anyway, I wanted to know why it felt so natural to live a lifestyle so alien to what society accepts. In regression, I experienced a society where multimate marriages seemed to be the order of the day. We all wore togas. The buildings were white, open, and it was warm. Maybe Atlantis or a country on the Mediterranean." He shrugged. "It was a happy, loving, open society. I was a female living with three other females and two males. I guess you'd call it polyfidelity today."

5.

"I have a hard time reconciling religion and an open sexual attitude," said Lorraine, a woman in her late thirties.

"Whose religion?" I said.

"All the major religions seem to repress sexuality."

"The Pagan religions—Celtic Druidism, Asatra and Wicca have existed far longer than Christianity, and have few sexual taboos. They believe it is wrong to have sex with someone who is in a monogamous relationship, or to cause unwanted pregnancy or spread sexual disease. But even sex outside of a committed relationship is acceptable if it fulfills the Pagan ethic of 'An it harm none, do as you will.'

I continued, "In Zen Buddhism, sex is included in the 'Three Pillars of Dharma' under Moral Restraint and is explained as refraining from actions of sensuality which cause pain and harm to others, or turbulence or disturbance in ourselves.

"Adultery is one of the precepts in the Six Paramitas of the

Bodhisattva. It is explained as meaning that the person having sex with another must consider his own happiness, that of his companion and of the third person who will be most affected by his action. If these three concerned people can be satisfied, then the sex act comes under natural law and is completely acceptable."

"I would like to think that way," Lorraine said. "In this life at age ten, my mother caught me masturbating, and she took me to the parish priest who made me do penance. From then on, when I attended mass and he looked at me, I knew he was thinking about it. It's why I rejected the church when I went to college."

"You know now that masturbating wasn't wrong. Accept that your beliefs have been programmed by a church whose teachings you no longer accept."

She nodded.

"Accept karmic responsibility, and let go of the blame and guilt. In daily meditation, say, 'I know the cause of my sexual viewpoint and I release the effect.' Chant it as a mantra. Then forgive yourself, and forgive your mother, and the priest, and the church. Send them all white light and let go. Also, fully explore your emotions and beliefs about sex, and about who you are and what you want. Awareness can lead to liberation."

6.

"A sexually open attitude is one thing, but polyfidelity just isn't acceptable," said Diane, a stocky woman in her forties. She held one hand on her hip as she spoke.

"Study history, and you'll find that polygamy has often been more common than monogamy. But I'm concerned with the present. Nearly half the people who read my magazine and attend my seminars are single; many are looking for and not finding the right mate. Others are unhappily married. Then consider the divorce rate and the number of single parents. Relationships and family units are destined to take many different forms as we move into the next century."

7.

"In a time of AIDS, endorsing multimate relationships is absolutely irresponsible," said Frank, Diane's husband.

"Statistically, AIDS has not significantly altered the bedding habits of singles, nor have married people ceased having affairs. For some of these people, pledging monogamy to a safe group might be the most responsible consideration."

"But you're arguing that it's more desirable to be non-monogamous."

"No, Frank. I support the right for everyone to choose what works best for them. Remove the stigma and labels. Monogamy is okay. Consensual non-monogamy is okay. Polyfidelity is okay. Triads are okay. All equally okay."

Monogamy

A monogamous marriage is obviously the relationship choice of the majority of the population. If monogamy works for you, I can see no reason to explore alternatives that might alter the existing dynamic. The following quotes and excerpts are not intended to demean monogamy, but to share some alternative ideas and approaches to relationships.

W. Brugh Joy, M.D. is a spiritual teacher, who wrote *Joy's Way—A Map for the Transformational Journey.* The book changed hundreds of thousands of lives. A decade later, he wrote *Avalanche*, chronicling his spiritual evolution and exploring many aspects of life, including monogamy:

"... I have come to doubt that the human being is intrinsically monogamous. Monogamy feels to me like an ideal superimposed on reality or a defense against forces beyond the control of the rational and intellectual selves. Ample evidence exists that the human being functions very well in polygamous social settings. In societies such as those in Italy, which have withdrawn civil sanctions against divorce, multiple sexual relationships are freely explored. Of course, these relationships were going on all the time anyway. Our mouths, under the control of the mind, say one thing while our bodies go right ahead and live the suchness of life."

In the book, *Words From A Man Of No Words,* Bhagwan Shree Rajneesh said, "Why be confined to one love? Why force yourself to be confined to one love?—because nature does not intend it so.

"Nature intends you to know love in as many ways as possible, because what you can know from one woman you cannot know from another woman. What you can know and experience from one man will not be experienced with another man.

"Each love is unique.

"There is no competition.

"There is no quarrel."

Multimate Relationships

In her book, *Love Without Limits*, Dr. Deborah Anapol explores responsible non-monogamy and the quest for sustainable intimate relationships, by offering relationship models which replace the destructive marriage-divorce-remarriage cycle with ethical and responsible multipartner relating.

Historically and cross-culturally, nonmonogamy has not been the only legitimate choice, and it's likely that we're doing irreparable damage to our human ecosystems by trying to force all sexualoving relationships into the monogamous mold. Dr. Anapol convincingly maintains that instead, we would be better off determining when and for whom nonmonogamy is appropriate and then embracing it fully, openly and honestly. "Our exclusive monogamous culture enshrines jealousy and possessiveness. Instead of working to eliminate jealousy and possessiveness so that people can freely choose how they will mate, our civilization tends to establish cultural and moral barriers that eliminate legitimate alternatives," says Deborah.

Types of Alternative Relationships
(From "Love Without Limits")

Primary relationship: Lovers who are in a long-term, committed, marriage-type relationship are *primary partners*. Usually primary partners live together and share finances, parenting and decision-making. Primary partners are not necessarily legally married, but they *are* bonded together as a family.

Secondary relationship: Secondary partners may also have a long-term committed sexualoving relationship. But usually they live separately, have separate finances and see themselves as close friends rather than immediate family. Secondary partners may take on roles in each other's families similar to those of aunts and uncles in an extended family of blood relations.

Tertiary relationship: Lovers who spend time together only once in a while or for a brief time. Their contact may be very intimate, but they are not an important part of each other's day-to-day life.

Responsible nonmonogamy can be practiced by any number of partners in any combination of primary, secondary, and tertiary relationships. The diversity of form automatically creates a social environment different from our familiar homogeneous, avowedly monogamous culture. And this diversity of form challenges us to develop ethical guidelines which apply to the *quality* rather than the *form* of the relationship.

Forms of Responsible Nonmonogamy
(From "Love Without Limits")

Open marriage or open relationship: These are both non-exclusive couple relationships, the only difference being whether the couple is married or not. In this scenario, the partners have agreed that each can have outside sexualoving partners. A wide variety of ground rules and restrictions may apply.

Intimate network: This is a love style in which several ongoing secondary relationships coexist. Sometimes all members of the group eventually become lovers. Sometimes individuals have only two or three partners within the group. The group can include singles only, couples only, or a mixture of both. Another way to describe it would be as a circle of sexualoving friends.

Group marriage or multilateral marriage: These are both committed, long-term, primary relationships which include three or more adults in a marriage-like relationship. A group marriage can be open or closed to outside sexual partners.

Triad: Three sexualoving partners who may all be secondary, all be primary, or two may be primary with a third secondary. It can be open or closed. A triad can be heterosexual or homosexual, it is often the choice of two same-sex bisexuals and an opposite-sex heterosexual.

(NOTE: For information on *Love Without Limits* and Deborah's work see the Selected Biography.)

The Setting Free

In the end, for any kind of a relationship to be free, all partners must maintain their integrity and individuality while, through their union, increase the potential to be all they can be.

On the last page of *You Were Born Again To Be Together*, I said, "Being totally idealistic, what would 'real love' be like? To begin with, it could not be diminished by anything the other person said or did. Your love would not be dependent upon being loved. You would give freely, without any expectation of return. In an environment of "real love," you would allow total freedom to your mate, expecting no more than the other could give. You would love for what the other was. You would not expect your mate to change, to be something he or she was not. You would find joy in the other's happiness. To 'really love' someone, you need to be complete within yourself, and without fear. You will then find joy in the positive aspects of your relationship and allow the negatives to simply flow through you, without affecting you."

* * * * *

In an attempt to attain this ideal level of love, here are a few tenets to illuminate the path:

RESPECT DIFFERENCES: You and your partner(s) have different needs, motivations, goals, and dreams. Treasure each other's uniqueness and accept each other as you are without expectations of change.

TRUST: To trust others, you must trust yourself. When you can trust without expectations, you integrate your fears. In any relationship, trust is built one encounter at a time as the result of keeping agreements.

COMMITMENT: Totally commit to your relationship— mentally, physically, spiritually, emotionally, and financially. Withholding reflects doubts that will undermine the foundation of your union.

COMPASSION: Provide comfort to each other in the midst of worldly concerns. Be friends as well as lovers and let your union be a refuge of balance and harmony. In showing compassion, don't sacrifice yourself for it will create resentment. Know that whatever you do for others you really do for yourself. Then do it anyway.

DETACHMENT: Let the little things go. Before reacting negatively, ask yourself, "Does it really matter or am I just acting out of a need to be right?"

COMMUNICATION: Openly communicate and share yourself. The greatest gift you can give each other is to be all of who you are. Be willing to discuss needs and compromise solutions.

LISTEN: Listen to each other and be willing to appreciate the other's position even when you don't agree. Also, learn to hear what isn't being said—what your partner(s) is feeling and needing. Know what you need, ask for it directly, and make it all right for your partner(s) to say no.

TIME: Always make time for each other. Shared activities are the building blocks of a good relationship (activities in addition to sex and watching TV). Remember too, everyone needs time alone.

TRANSCEND ANGER: Release anger by saying to yourself, "I am angry because I didn't get what I want. I had expectations of approval or control, and this isn't my right."

SPIRITUALITY: Encourage each other to evolve spiritually by helping each other to integrate fear-based emotions. Through expanded awareness you can transcend the darkness and attain peace of mind.

CHAPTER 10

VERY CONTROVERSIAL SUBJECTS

Resolving karma is a matter of being responsible to yourself. The underlying thrust behind the human-potential movement is openness, honesty, and self-responsibility. From a higher perspective we may all be one, but from a day-to-day karmic perspective, your goal is to evolve individually.

Man cannot create anything higher than his own level of understanding. So, society cannot evolve beyond the level of the masses. It all starts and ends with individuals. Hopefully, masses of caring, self-actualized individuals will ultimately generate a higher psychological and spiritual level than we are presently experiencing.

It is through the assertion of your own will and personality that you will attain freedom of the self and from the self. It follows that the interests of the individual should take precedence over the interests of the state or any social group. Peaceful coexistence and a civilized society can only be achieved by recognizing individual rights.

Historically, the idea of "greater good" has served as the moral justification for all social programs and all tyrannies. Greater good is only accomplished through the violation of individual rights—a price too high to pay, especially if you're the one paying it.

My support of individual rights is echoed in my long-term support of the American Civil Liberties Union (whose sole purpose is to support the U.S. Constitution and laws of this land). This and other positions have generated emotional responses from many readers. My answers to questions about earth changes and alternatives to society-approved marriage (both covered in other chapters), gurus, environmentalism and diet have generated thousands of letters. If you're tempted to write in protest, please know that I've probably already read it many times.

Against Universal Law?

Since the early '80s, when Ronald Reagan was elected with the help of the religious right, I have been publicly vocal about my concerns over this fundamentalist movement. In 1986, Jesse Helms was attempting to remove Wicca's non-profit status, and all over the country politicians were sponsoring laws attempting to legislate New Age practices out of existence. In response, I spoke out loudly in *Master of Life* and *What Is* magazines, and in print and broadcast interviews. Eighty-five percent of my readers approved. The remainder did not. Today, the religious right is active again, and their agenda hasn't changed. The following letter and response from *What Is* seems appropriate again.

Q.

This is no time for the metaphysical community to give these people, or anyone interested in bringing about an Armageddon, any energy. We ought to be about our Father's business, bringing in the New Age. We can't use worldly methods or we will lose. Our anger and fear will feed their cause. Those of us with this thought probably do not realize how strong a force we are. If we use that force in anger or fear, how can we help but draw to us the same Armageddon our foe desires to create?

Whether you call universal power God, The Christ, or simply "What Is," I believe that Power is sending its "mother energy" into the world, at this time, to prepare for the birth of the New Age. Before birth, labor comes to a crescendo of pain. During the height of the pain, it may seem as though it will never end. But if you relax, breathe deeply, push when it is called for, and keep your mind on the wonderful goal, all of a sudden the miracle of life has occurred again. If you hold back or resist, you hurt the baby and yourself. Just when there seems to be no relief, the universe has intervened and you have drawn to you what you have created.

Please don't work against Universal law.

A.

My response to our antagonists is not going against Universal Law, nor is it feeding their cause. We are living on the earth so we must use "worldly" methods combined with spiritual.

To bring positive change, we must use positive action. But when we stop questioning and speaking out against the things we feel strongly about, we give permission for our rights to be taken away.

There is a metaphysical axiom that says, "You can't change what you don't recognize." All too many good people don't recognize what is happening. That is why I'm speaking out. Those who would oppress everything New Age would like nothing better than for us to remain quiet, apathetic and indifferent.

I do not advocate resistance with force, which would be alien to everything I believe in. Send our antagonists light and love ... and share, alert and network. We don't need to do this with malice or subversive tactics. It can be done very positively.

Look at history and you'll find that indifference and apathy have never worked in response to oppression. Believing as you do, you may not be apathetic or indifferent, but ignoring the threat leads to the same end result. Some wiser men than I have had some enlightening things to say about this:

"The death of democracy is not likely to be an assassination

from ambush. It will be a slow extinction from apathy, indiffer-ence, and undernourishment." —**Robert Maynard Hutchins, American educator**

"Indifference and apathy have one name—betrayal." —**Sal-vatore Quasimodo, Nobel Prize Winner**

"Philosophy should always know that indifference is a militant thing. It batters down the walls of cities and murders the women and children amid the flames and purloining of altar vessels. When it goes away, it leaves smoking ruins, where lie citizens bayonetted through the throat. It is not a children's pastime like mere highway robbery." —**Stephen Crane, American novelist**

Scary Movies Are Good For You

Here's an idea inspired by Dr. Brugh Joy that's sure to upset a few purists: Horror films will improve your life! Murder mysteries will balance your energy! Gory TV emergency-room shows may keep you from ending up in ER!

Before you object too loudly, hear me out. This is a three-part equation:

1. Physicists tell us the Universe (and all energy) functions as a yin/yang balance resulting in tension between opposites. Yin is negative, yang is positive. We all contain these dual aspects: love/hate, harmony/chaos, good/evil. Intuitively you know you must express your yin/yang duality, because this tension is necessary for structure to exist. Human beings are structure ... energy. And without tension, you don't exist. Dr. Brugh Joy explains it by saying, "Life seeks to be fully expressed."

For just a moment, don't think of positive as good and negative as bad, because "the balance" doesn't label. In an automobile battery, the plates are alternated, positive and negative, and the tension between them generates energy. The positive plate isn't a "good" plate and the negative isn't "bad." They just are.

The most common expressions of yin energy are arguing,

fighting, frustration, anxiety, self-denial, excess hard work, gambling, dangerous activities, accidents, extramarital affairs, drugs, drinking, and illness, from a common cold to a terrible disease. War is the ultimate expression of yin energy.

2. Extensive reality/fantasy tests have shown by recording brain waves that the subconscious (programming portion of your mind) does not distinguish between imagined events and real experiences. If you watch a woman dance while your brain waves are monitored, a unique pattern will be recorded. Any other experience will generate a totally different pattern. But if you vividly imagine the woman dancing, your brain waves will generate the exact same pattern as created by the real experience.

3. The most common expressions of yin energy do not serve you. But a scary movie, or a horrific book just might help life to "fully express itself" in a harmless way. Afterwards, you can avoid an argument or skip a cold.

Some spiritual seekers are so blissed-out they can hardly function in society. They may be spiritual, but their lives are a mess. They eat no meat. They block all angry thoughts. They meditate by the hour. They espouse peace and harmony. And they've repressed their yin energy to the point of becoming lopsided ... dysfunctional.

Gurus condemn society and encourage this kind of mental bliss, because they need loyal supporters. The argument isn't valid. We reincarnated to schoolhouse earth to interact with society ... to be tested by the times. (To understand the real nature of the mental bliss, see the "brainwashing" chapter in this book.)

Environmentalism
Q.

As a progressive metaphysical publication, you should support environmentalism. Why do you ignore these issues?

A.

You should see my mail. Others want me to be concerned about UFO abductions or the fate of Public Radio. Some women in Oregon are determined to talk me into writing metaphysical books for teenagers. Born Again Christians want to convert me. A white supremacist organization thinks I should share their ideas (their mail goes to the FBI).

Environmentalist? Anyone who isn't concerned about air, water and food pollution has to be brain dead, but I'm suspicious of many environmental "truths" and the motives behind green communications. Environmentalism tends to attract some pretty militant people who accept the propaganda as gospel.

Any successful mass movement, which environmentalism has become, has to exaggerate and omit much. Environmentalism is currently a socially and politically correct cause. But here are a just a few facts that make me nervous about the rest of the green's agenda:

Landfills: Greens say that nonbiodegradable products are bad. But in reality, for two-thirds of the nation's landfills (those without liners), it's the degradable products that pose an environmental threat. Degradation can lead to leaching, and as chemicals reach the water supply they can pose a health threat. Sealed landfills allow very little degradation of any kind, so your choices regarding degradability don't matter.

Diapers: Consumers who care mainly about landfills may choose cloth diapers. But consumers who care more about air and water pollution and conserving water and energy might choose disposables. In their life cycle, cloth diapers consume six times more water than disposables, and require three times as much energy. The production and use of disposables generates about a tenth of the amount of air and water pollution.

Recycling: Sometimes it makes sense and sometimes it doesn't. Curbside recycling programs often require more collection trucks, which use more fuel and cause more air pollution. Some recycling programs use large amounts of energy and produce high volumes of waste water. Unless the recycling plant is nearby, it requires considerable resources just to transport the materials.

Trees: In the USA, the trees used to make paper are grown explicitly for that purpose, so if we recycle more paper, fewer trees will be planted and grown by commercial harvesters. The net effect of recycling could be a decline in tree planting and tree coverage of the earth.

Plastics: Greens hate plastic. Yet plastics take less energy to manufacture than aluminum or glass. A German organization researched the effects of eliminating plastic packaging in that country. Result: energy consumption would nearly double and the weight of solid wastes would increase 404 percent.

Ozone depletion: There is no ozone depletion and ultraviolet rays are decreasing at all cities measured, not increasing. According to news reports and *The Hole in the Ozone Scare*, a new book by scientists Rogelio Madufo and Ralf Schauerhammer, some bad science and fear-mongering environmental groups caused unnecessary panic. There's a lot to the story, but in short, the NASA Ozone Report was kept secret for almost three years after the announcement of the findings—so it wasn't peer reviewed. To put the report in perspective, understand that there is a natural one-year ozone cycle in which the amount of ozone peaks and declines. To get the results showing the decrease between 1969 and 1985, the researchers used a peak measurement in 1969 and the trough measurement in 1985.

According to Norwegian scientific research, "... the so-called ozone hole in Antarctica is a transient springtime depletion." And even if the ozone were depleting, placing the blame on chlorofluorocarbons (CFCs) doesn't work, because they are destroyed in the lower atmosphere. And even if the CFCs were somewhat responsible, the report doesn't mention Mt. Erebus, an Antarctica volcano located only 10 kilometers upwind from the depletion-measurement site. The volcano releases 50 times as much chlorine into the stratosphere as the entire annual breakup of CFCs.

In 1975 a major environmental concern was echoed in the pages of the *New York Times:* "Many signs point to the possibility that the earth may be heading for another ice age." *Science* magazine in 1976 said we were heading "toward extensive Northern Hemisphere glaciation." *Global Ecology* in 1971 said we were facing "continued rapid cooling of the earth." *Science* in 1975 called it "the approach of a full-blown 10,000-year ice age." Wrong on all counts.

According to George F. Will, "Ecopessimism persists, more solid than environmental science, in part because it serves a political program. Some environmentalism is a 'green tree with red roots.' It is the socialist dream—ascetic lives closely regulated by a vanguard of bossy visionaries—dressed up as compassion for the planet."

Pornography

Q.

I have a strong craving for pornography and would like to know if this could be an obstacle in my attempting to become a Master of Life.

A.

Metaphysical purists would tell you to transmute this desire into something "higher." This is the idea of spiritual alchemy—to change the structure of the desire vibration into a higher frequency through intensified mental focus. It sounds great, and an advanced yogi may be able to do it, but for most it's just an exercise in repression.

Behavioral therapists might tell you to go ahead and read or watch porno, and just as you're getting excited, shock yourself with a buzzer, or use thought-stopping techniques. The danger here is shutting down your sexual responses entirely.

Jimmy Swaggart would probably tell you to pray away your craving, but that didn't seem to work too well for him.

The "everything is a disease" folks would tell you to attend a 12-step program, such as Sex Addicts Anonymous.

Metaphysical poet William Blake (were he still alive), might tell you that "indulgence will lead you to the palace of wisdom."

I would remind you of a few things: Everything you are attracted to is the *natural* result of past programming in this life or a past life (or both). It is karmic, so there is something to be learned from it. Once you have the awareness to ask the right questions, you can probably find your own answers.

Advice: If you are upset by unacceptable things, all you have to do to resolve the situation is accept what seems unacceptable. Examine these aspects of your life until you understand they exist as a personal issue only because you give them power. You empower them by choosing to view them in a certain way.

In other words, since your craving for pornography doesn't hurt anyone else, to free yourself, accept what is. To try to directly change the situation is usually a waste of time. It doesn't work or it makes matters worse. In this case you would begin to repress your needs, which will always surface in one form or another, and maybe as perversion.

Action: Take a long look at your sexual "aliveness" with your sex partner(s). If real-life sex were more stimulating, maybe you'd be less attracted to pornography. If you aren't sexually active, put some energy into becoming active with a partner who shares your tastes. Although it may take some effort, it can be done.

Dale Carnegie

Q.

Why don't you incorporate some of the fantastic teachings of Dale Carnegie into your seminars? He changed my life more effectively than any metaphysical seminar ever could.

A.

The Carnegie Course teaches you to say what will work to get what you want. Isn't that being a phoney or a hypocrite? Forget sincerity. Forget honesty. Forget being real. Carnegie teaches you to be a diplomat and wear a mask. Masks are the fear that who and what you are isn't adequate, so you pretend to be somebody else. Yes, you may *win friends and influence people* who will be there for you as long as you pretend to be who they want you to be. Isn't that allowing yourself to be manipulated? Do you need any relationship or association that badly?

Masks are also **repression** and there is always a price to pay. In my seminars, I often say, "Repression is like a rubber boat. You can hold it under water as long as you're willing to exert effort, but eventually you'll get tired and it will surface." Repression surfaces in different ways. One person develops a skin rash, someone else gets ulcers, another takes it out on his mate by starting a fight, and yet another represses for years and eventually manifests cancer.

When you are direct and honest in your communications and in your life, there is no need to wear masks and no need for repression ... which translates as "no fear."

Q.

Have you actually taken the Dale Carnegie course? I thought, as a metaphysical person, one is supposed to remember not to judge others. Were you just in a bad mood when you answered that gentleman asking why you didn't incorporate Carnegie concepts into your seminars? Come on, please let me know.

A.

Not judging others does not mean that you ignore faults or

mistakes. You don't turn off your brain and stop deciding what works and what doesn't. I don't need to experience the Japanese Hell Camp Training in the U.S.A. to know it is alien to all I teach. I don't need to experience punk rock concerts, tuna-banana pie or communism to know they don't work for me. Am I being spiritually judgmental? Hopefully, you haven't stopped deciding what works for you and what doesn't.

No, I haven't taken the Carnegie course. My words are based upon reading Carnegie's books (the basis of his course) and my personal contacts with many, many Dale Carnegie graduates. I used to make a game of asking, "By any chance are you a Dale Carnegie graduate?" I was never wrong.

To rise above fear, you take off your masks. There are thousands of masks: An honest and dependable mask you put on for your boss. A nicey-nicey smiling mask is worn when you want people to like you. A good-time Charlie gregarious mask can deflect real contact or intimacy, or cover insecurity. And there are martyr masks, quiet masks, superiority masks, I-can-handle-anything masks, indifference masks, *ad infinitum*.

When you wear a mask, the fear is that being who you really are won't get you what you want. So, to make the impression that will get you what you want, you pretend to be someone else. Enter Dale Carnegie, whose book *How To Win Friends & Influence People* has sold 16 million copies. It features such sections as: "The Six Ways to *Make* People Like You" (emphasis mine), and "The Nine Ways To Change People Without Arousing Resentment." The whole book is about manipulating the other guy so you can get what you want—for them to like you, to agree with you, or to buy or sell a particular service or goods.

Samples of key phrases: "Encourage others to talk about themselves." "Make the other person feel important." "Let the other person feel that the idea is his or hers." "Appeal to their nobler motives."

As I asked last issue, what about sincerity, honesty, being

real? If you use Carnegie techniques to win friends, the friendship has to be based upon a two-way manipulation. You pretend to be the mask to attain the friendship and they will be your friend as long as you wear it. What happens when your mask slips and they find out who you really are? Do you need any relationship or association so badly that you're willing to repress your real self in order to attain it?

I realize that most people respond very positively to the Carnegie form of communication. I don't. There is nothing I want enough to sacrifice that much self-esteem.

Space Brothers

Q.

You seem to be totally silent about UFOs, alien abductions and the important communications that are being received from space beings. Don't you accept this? Do you care?

A.

I make it a practice not to waste my time or energy on something I can do nothing about (abductions). Until I can, I'll remain focused upon human relationships, which each of us can do plenty about. In regard to the communications: it's the same message that spiritual channels have been reporting for years. Lately, even Australian aborigines have (supposedly) gotten into the act. We must stop fighting and stop polluting, love ourselves and love our neighbors, and if we don't, we're going to destroy mankind. Got it.

Politics

Q.

After reading your magazine for over two years, I think you're a liberal Democrat. A friend who is equally familiar with your writings swears you're a conservative Republican. Who is right?

A.

Conservatives (A) support the opportunities of capitalism and the right to enjoy the benefits of your labors, but (B) they want to dictate your lifestyle and force you to accept their values.

Liberals (A) support individual rights and free thinking, but (B) they want to coerce social parity and distribute your resources to serve their view of the greater good.

To me, the goals of freedom *of* the self and *from* the self are in keeping with the A aspects of both schools of thought, but I reject the B aspects as unacceptable. The conservative's desire to integrate church and state, and their anti-gay, anti-abortion, anti-minority, positions are unacceptable. The liberals' penchant for quotas, excessive taxation and throwing money at social problems are unacceptable.

The answer is neither. I vote candidate by candidate. But most repulsive to me is the conservative desire to legislate morality and integrate church and state. The upcoming exploration of resentment against achievement explores another aspect of political concern.

Historic Resentment

The following, like it or not, is a historic pattern that challenges us to integrate spirituality and reality.

As a society evolves, resentment against the middle and upper classes (bourgeois) increases. Responsible society—those who work hard for a living—are blamed by the proletariat (the unpropertied, or poorest people) for all their problems, who at the same time demand equality. Those who have contributed least to the growth develop strong resentments when they find themselves lacking the benefits attained by those who have worked hard, saved and taken chances. The resentment builds into envy and hatred, and the higher the civilization rises, the more intense the negative proletarian emotions become.

When the middle and upper classes of a society identify with the morality of achievement, such resentments will accurately be viewed primarily as complaints of the lazy and undisciplined. Economic growth will not be affected. But if the successful identify with this resentment-morality, they will begin to feel guilty about their accomplishments. Historically, this guilt and resentment-morality has also been reinforced by religions that admonish "give up your worldly goods."

Religion, with its resentment of material success and its promotion of suffering and guilt, succeeded in reversing economic growth after the fall of the Roman Empire, plunging mankind into the Dark Ages. Today, these same values repress the lives of millions, including entire countries. People sacrifice achievement in this life for the promise of a glorious afterlife.

Robert Sheaffer, in *Resentment Against Achievement*, says, "During difficult times, all activity that results in economic growth is generally welcomed as a positive contribution to the general welfare. A period dominated by respect for achievement begins. However, as economic growth accelerates, the industrious people primarily responsible for that growth inevitably accumulate considerable private wealth. In circumstances where people are not allowed to keep the wealth they generate, as for example, in socialist countries, or in tribal societies, economic growth grinds to a halt. As living conditions gradually improve, people become less concerned about day-to-day survival and become increasingly envious of the very visible wealth that some people in their midst enjoy."

Historically, achievers generate so much proletariat envy, resentment becomes stronger than the desire for continued economic growth. A period of resentment begins. Even if everyone in the society is experiencing a rising standard of living, if the achievers' lifestyle is improving faster, it triggers profound resentment. Revolution is often the result, and those of wealth are imprisoned or murdered. Some societies pass laws confiscating and redistributing the wealth. Either way, economic progress grinds to a halt and everyone experiences a reduced standard of living. After a few months, years or decades of hard times, the populace comes to the conclusion that economic growth is needed. Resentment fades and an era of achievement can begin again.

Spiritual Diet

Some vegetarians are "true believers" in the mold of the most radical Born-Again Christians or environmentalists. They have the one-and-only answer and woe be unto anyone who suggests they don't. True no-meat, no-fish, no-poultry, no-dairy vegetarians make up only a tiny percentage of the population. But they fill my mail box with angry protests every time I've mentioned in print to some dietary indiscretion. Usually, I'm told that such-and-such book will save my sinful soul. Of course, the author is also a vegetarian true believer and can hardly be considered objective. Like all true believers, the super-vegetarians need to be occasionally reminded that **we live in a democracy.**

The following is an excerpt from a *Master of Life Winners* article that had a good number of vegetarians threatening to "slaughter" me.

The New Healers
Diet and The Chemistry of Metaphysics

Sheree Becker ("The Healing Space" columnist) had been telling me about Dr. Terry Dulin for months. "He's an ortho-molecular biochemist practicing on Long Island. Medically, he's years ahead of his time," she said. "Using his own blood-work formulas to prescribe diet and supplements, he is saving people that medical doctors and Park Avenue psychiatrists had given up on." Sheree felt Terry had "saved her life."

163

The more "Dulin" stories I heard, the more fascinated I became. The man used diet, vitamins and specific amino acids to rework an individual's DNA. The opportunity to meet Terry came while conducting our Professional Past-Life Therapy Hypnotist Training in Terrytown, New York. Sheree was on the support team and suggested she invite Terry for dinner.

When the evening arrived, I was tired after a day of working intensely with the seminar participants. I told Tara, "Let's make it a quick dinner so we can get to bed early."

The dinner lasted until 4 A.M., because we encouraged Terry to keep talking by asking endless questions. Finally exhausted, I asked him to stay over and allow me to tape record more of what he had to say. He agreed.

One of the most interesting things Terry talked about was the ability to predict behavior by diet—even the behavior of nations. I mentioned our love of Mexican food. He said, "But if you ate that diet all the time, it wouldn't work for you. Beans, corn tortillas, tomatoes, salt—histamine and tryptophan. Predictably, you'd swing from being laid back to highly emotional."

He went on to explain that when you eat food high in histamine, your adrenaline elevates to balance it. The more histamine foods you eat, the higher your adrenaline. Push your adrenaline high enough, you make yourself crazy. "High adrenaline people are psychotic," he said. "When they really get out of control, they become violent—they're angry, irritated people who have no logic centers." I thought of the high histamine diet so prevalent in South Central Los Angeles and wondered if it was a contributing factor in the riots.

Terry talked about the "chemistry of metaphysics," explaining the validity of palmistry as a reflection of your specific DNA code, and went on to discuss our seminar audience. He had spent the better part of the day sitting in on the seminar sessions, and explained that after years of relating people to their blood work he could read chemical makeup in people's faces. "They're all high glutamines (an amino acid)," he said. "Glutamine is naturally high in women, which makes them more intuitive. Every psychic I've seen a blood scan on has elevated glutamine. Every single one. The more glutamine, the more psychic they are."

I asked if this might have something to do with so many of the best male psychics being gay. Terry agreed that it fit the pattern. I asked if avoiding meats and eating lots of breads and pastas, which would increase glutamine, would also increase psychic ability. The answer was yes, but he advised against such dietary practice.

After listening to some incredible case histories in which Terry had quite literally saved the "unsaveable"—drug addicts, suicidal people, uncontrollable hyperactive children—I said, "If you can do that can you help me lower my cholesterol?"

He laughed.

I explained, "We eat a diet of whole-grain breads, low-fat yogurt, cheese, fish, some lean chicken and turkey, vegetables and fruits."

"The typical New Age diet," he said.

I nodded. "My cholesterol is border-line—239. My doctor wants it to come down. He's nixed butter, eggs, and meat, but I can't seem to budge the numbers more than a point or two."

Terry said, "If you really want to reduce your cholesterol, eat two eggs a day, meat twice a day, with plenty of fresh fruits and vegetables. No breads. No dairy. Once I read your blood, I'll tell you what meats, vegetables and fruits, and I'll prescribe specific amino acids and vitamins."

"Huh?"

"Eat a lot of plums, blueberries, mangos, papaya," he continued and provided some additional advice.

Back home in California the whole family had their blood drawn, and we all followed Terry's advice. Two weeks later, before receiving any word from Terry, I needed to have a blood test as part of an insurance examination. My cholesterol was already down to 219—a twenty point drop. Then I received Terry's diet: turkey four times a week, beef three, pork three, chicken three, veal once, fish once. Daily: two eggs, two cups of vegetables from my list, five fruits from my list and a cup of cashews a week. Plus he prescribed a high dosage list of individual vitamins and specific amino acids. (*NOTE: This was my diet formula, based upon my blood work. Other people are assigned very different programs. Random use of amino acids can cause severe problems.*)

Four weeks later, my cholesterol was 198 and I'd lost ten pounds. And I was no longer taking the antacids I so often needed for an upset stomach.

Tara had always leaned a little more toward vegetarianism than I. The thought of eating meat horrified her. Terry said he could set it up as a vegetarian diet, but it was complicated and would require a lot of dedication. Plus she'd be eating more nuts than squirrels. Since she was the primary cook, she decided to go along with me and our three children, although there were many differences in our diets. For example, she was to eat beef only twice a week, and fish twice. Her mega-vitamin program and amino acids were also different.

Tara's results were similar to mine. Her cholesterol dropped to where it belonged. Terry wanted her to retain her existing weight, but to gain some strength, so he built that into the formula.

My son Hunter's blood indicated future health problems if changes weren't made immediately. He naturally tended toward kefirs, yogurts and grains, eating as little protein as he could get by with. Six weeks after the dietary change we noticed positive behavioral changes in both Hunter and our daughter Cheyenne. But what a battle it was to get them to give up their morning cereal and kefir for eggs and fruit. Years later, they're still talking about breakfasts in the good old days before Dr. Dulin.

Soon, several of our friends wanted Dulin to analyze their

blood and prescribe diets. Most were writers or in the entertainment business, and all had similar results. A Universal Studio screen writer, with a background in biochemistry, was so impressed with his dietary results, he stopped writing scripts to work with Terry on a book.

I asked Terry more questions about cholesterol. He said, "You cannot absorb more than .5 grams a day of cholesterol, end of story. If you eat a bowl of it a day it doesn't make any difference. I give my cardiac patients beef, eggs, pork. They eat meat like crazy, but I cut out all the grains. And they turn around and their cholesterol drops anywhere from 20 to 50 points in less than two months."

"Why do *they* keep telling everybody not to eat protein?" I asked.

Terry shrugged. "What that's going to do is weaken your immune system, weaken your brainpower, weaken your muscles, weaken everything. They keep saying to eat carbohydrates and not to eat protein, which makes no sense, unless someone wants a sluggish, depressed population."

Typical Response
Q.

Shame, shame, shame for pushing the pro-meat industry-diet-lifestyle. How dare you toxify our world? How can you glorify the killing, cannibalizing of our warm-hearted, living, breathing animal friends? Why do you eat your friends? WAKE UP! I am sick to my stomach.

A.

The magazine story resulted from my own, my family's and friend's experience. Being true, maybe we need to question conventional dietary wisdom.

As an addendum: I recently went to a respected, holistic doctor/acupuncturist in Malibu after straining my back from over-exercise at the gym. After examining me, he said, "You used to be a vegetarian, but not for the last year or so."

He explained how muscle breaks down without meat protein, and told me he had once been a serious vegetarian who balanced his diet to maximize the benefits. He gave it up because of problems with his own muscles and what he learned about the sad physical state of his vegetarian patients.

I don't advocate that anyone give up vegetarianism for an egg/meat eating diet. But one diet doesn't fit all, as a lot of health writers would have you believe. Many aspects of meat-eating concerns me, as I wrote about in *Unseen Influences*. So I'm still interviewing, experimenting and investigating, and buying my meat from a holistic grocery that guarantees no hormone and drug additives have been fed to the animals.

In response to the "cannibalizing" of animals raised for food, Tara and I, and dozens of spiritual people working in this field, all accept that the animals were incarnated for that purpose.

NOTE: The final paragraph of my response really did it. I received dozens of letters saying things like, "I'd like to slaughter you, for saying that." "You deserve to be butchered and grilled, you *!@#*!!." Such loving, non-aggressive spiritual sentiments to encourage me to join the vegetarian cause!

After discussing this volume of negative letters with Terry, he sent me the following to share with my readers.

Dr. Terry Dulin's Response

Since the vegetarians are up in arms about your "New Healers" article and some things that I said, I think I should clarify what I meant and a little more about my system.

First, I am not anti-vegetarianism. Having a chemistry background, I don't see vegetables, meats, nuts, seeds, or any other foods as they exist on the plate. My point of view is one of physiology. Your stomach doesn't really care if it is fed a piece of red meat or a hand full of nuts; it only sees the chemical composition found in the food. The basic components of fats, carbohydrates and proteins are all the body cares about. This can be from any source, including a nutrient paste—such as the type astronauts use, which is probably a better source of nutrients for humans than anything else, (although it has as much appeal as cod liver oil). Whether it is from an animal or vegetable source, any diet can be balanced by the basic components. Having many vegetarian patients in my practice (nearly 100 at last count), we don't force them to eat meat, but rather make sure they are balancing the basics and promoting good health. You see, even a vegetarian diet can be destructive in the long run, if it is not in balance with the individual's own specific body chemistry.

Many of the vegetarians I have seen over the years are not really true vegetarians but fall into several groups. The first is the pathological group of people who use vegetarian behaviors to hide an eating disorder or some other emotionally based illness. The second group is what I call "vegetable eaters." They tend to eat nothing but fruit and vegetables, allowing the body to go into imbalance due to improper protein intake. The third group are those who use tremendous amounts of grains to balance their diet and for the most part are healthy, but have as well some minor imbalances due to following improper information they have read or heard by word of mouth. These are not true vegetarians.

The true vegetarians are those people who build their lifestyle around their diet and eat many different food groupings to make sure they have a total component of the necessary building blocks from their diet. These people are dedicated and very meticulous about eating many meals per day and they think out their food groups extensively. Much of their day is spent cooking and preparing meals. These people truly have the advantage of a good, balanced diet.

But is a vegetarian diet the best diet and one that everyone should follow? The answer to that is a simple no. Is a vegetarian diet a more spiritual diet? The answer to that is also no. Now that I have made some really inflammatory statements, let me back them up with logical thought.

Any diet that is not in the right balance for an individual is going to be destructive. If the necessary components are not found in the diet, the body will suffer and fall into a disease state. Since each individual is unique and has a unique chemical balance, the diet must match the person (not the person match the diet). This doesn't mean a vegetarian diet can't be made to balance out for each individual, but the individual may not have the time or energy to do what it takes to maintain a proper balance.

For example, a person who lives on Long Island and works in New York, may have to get up at 5 AM and run to make a 6:30 train. This gets them to their job at nine and then they are working until 1 PM, when they break for their one-hour lunch. They have enough time to get lunch, socialize for a bit and then back to work they go. When 5 PM rolls around they catch a train and return home by seven or eight at night. This grind goes on five days per week. That makes it very difficult to get up an hour earlier to cook brown rice for breakfast. Time is a big factor in a vegetarian lifestyle. The next problem, most people don't have access to vegetarian restaurants, so they end up eating a salad for lunch because they want to have some semblance of a social life. If they associate with people who are not vegetarians they invariably get stuck going to places where they can't get a complete vegetarian meal. As the week runs on, they fall further behind in their nutritional needs. If they brown bag it, they can keep up their nutrient status, but now they stay in for lunch and can't do much socializing. In addition, they now spend at least one whole day cooking and preparing meals for the week. This further cuts down on time. The lucky ones have a spouse who will take the time to do all the preparation while they work. So there are ways around this but most people are either too busy, tired or just plain lazy to do it right. Although, you must remember, I see mostly patients who have a problem and therefore I am not commenting on those who do it right with good results.

So, time factors and the need to make a living also play a part in the vegetarians lifestyle. These too must be taken into consideration when looking at balance for an individual. Several articles recently printed in some of the vegetarian magazines also play out this point. Many of the gurus have begun to add dairy and eggs to some of their followers' diets. This is because they realize that the quality of food is not the same as it was when the vegetarian regimes were originally set up. So, to compensate for the needs of the individual, they have allowed some animal products as a way to keep their followers healthy. This again is balancing the diet to the individual and not the individual to the diet. When looking at meat diets versus vegetarian diets you must take all of this into consideration. Meat diets have the advantage of being very nutrient-dense and require less quantity to be complete. Vegetarian diets require more work and higher volume. The choice is the individuals and not the chemistry. If you won't put in the time then you should eat more of a meat diet. But if you have the time and dedication for a vegetarian diet then by all means follow it.

Now that we have seen time and availability make a difference in the choice of diet (vegetarian vs. meat), lets take a look at some of the other arguments.

Some people believe that a high protein diet is cancer causing. This is a fallacy. Meat, which is not the only source of protein (nuts and seeds also contain high amounts of protein), do have artificial chemicals put into them. Yes, beef and pork are shot up with steroids and growth hormones. Plus chickens and turkeys are fed penicillin mold and marigold blossoms to improve juiciness and weight. Veal is treated inhumanely as are most commercial chickens which live in small cages stacked up on top of each other. So we all agree that animals used for food are not treated well.

But this will not change until consumers on a large scale switch to free-range chickens and beef. I almost forgot to mention fish. A noted sea explorer found fish in the middle of the Atlantic ocean with PCB based liver tumors (a toxin made from plastics). This is the result of pollution. But the toxins in meats and fish are only part of the toxins in the environment: Acid rains fall on crops of fruits and vegetables. DDT residuals are found in soil 40 to 50 years after their use. Much of the U.S. ground water used to irrigate crop land has toxins from industry in it. Many of the organic farms are found near roadways, and the pollution from the cars gives them a higher lead content. So to say that vegetables are clear of toxins is not true. In fact, the entire food chain is contaminated with pollutants in one form or another.

This sounds very bleak if you look only at the negatives. But the human body has wonderful tricks up its sleeve or in its liver. The liver has many chemical mechanisms for removing toxins and making them harmless. If you don't overuse one particular mechanism and if you keep the toxin intake evenly spread out, then your body can remove the toxins without much damage occurring. The old adage of everything in moderation and nothing in abundance is still a good rule of thumb. So by not restricting the body to one constant type of toxin, it has the best chance of cleaning itself out without major malfunctions or a burnout in the removal mechanism. So people who only consume one type of vegetable pattern (rice and beans) or one type of meat pattern (chicken and fish) are actually stressing the removal mechanisms for those specific toxins and probably opening themselves up for a burnout in the body's ability to handle that toxin.

To further complicate matters, as if the above mentioned items weren't enough, genetically engineered fruits and vegetables are beginning to appear on shelves. (The FDA approved this and

Vice President Dan Quayle allowed it to become law through the committee on commerce). Tomatoes with peanut proteins genetically placed in them are being distributed without identifying labels. Many other fruits and vegetables will undergo the same genetic alterations, all without anyone's knowledge. So you really can't tell if what you see is what you get. Plus, many farms are injecting fruits with sugar water to increase their sweetness. This adds another non-nature produced intervention in the food chain. As you can see, vegetables are becoming as tainted as the meat, with unknown effects on the human system.

It is my contention that vegetarians should think less about attacking meat eaters and instead attack those who are destroying our food chain right under our noses. Perhaps one day we will find the way to produce vegetable protein en masse and improve its density enough that the volume won't be needed. This will save the animals and keep the human body in balance. But until that day, we all need to do what will keep our individual systems running at optimum functionally, whether that be a meat or vegetarian diet.

Now on to the spiritual point. Many people believe that a vegetarian diet is the only way to be spiritual. This would mean that all vegetarians are spiritual and most meat eaters are not. So lets take a case in point: Gandhi was a vegetarian and he was very spiritual. Adolf Hitler was also a vegetarian and he was not very spiritual. So much for the diet making a person spiritual or not. I believe that there are certain human functions which are indeed chemical in nature. However, I do not believe spirituality is one of them.

Spirituality is the commitment of one's soul, higher consciousness if you will, to helping and not hurting humanity. It is encompassed in the small things, like a helping hand, a smile when someone is down, a hug for those in pain—as well as larger-scale compassion, such as feeding the poor, protecting animals, and saving the environment.

Each of us has a specific job in this existence and some of us need to do large things and others are slated for smaller tasks. But large or small, we are all part of a much greater whole—so much more than our consciousness can really understand. Change occurs by example, not by ridicule or anger. If each of us in our own way sets good spiritual examples, then the world would indeed change for the better.

You vegetarians who judge meat eaters as bad need to remember that the highest of High made this world in a very balanced state. Each death goes to the renewal of another. The death of a large animal in turn provides existence for the smaller ones and food for the insects' survival. Each species is intertwined in the dance of life and death. As we watch nature allow for the recycling of air and water, so is it the same with the animals big and small. Each returns its matter back to the pool so life can continue for another. Maybe vegetarians prevent the overgrowth of vegetation as meat eaters stop the overpopulation of animals. This keeps the balance and allows for all life to continue. Then again, maybe not. But if we all worked on our own optimum spiritual and physical health, the answers would become self-evident. —**Dr. Terence Dulin**

Q.

Even if what you say about Dr. Dulin's dietary approach is true, meat offers the lowest food vibration. We all need to eat higher on the vibrational food scale.

A.

This is your belief, not an absolute, revealed fact. You've read it and heard people say it who have heard people say it until it has become a "New Age Truth." What mystical Master determined the vibrations? Does he use an electronic food-vibration measuring device? Where can I buy one?

When someone from a large transcendental meditation community recently told me I had to get my vibrational-food act together, I asked how he knew that meat registered low on the scale. "It's common knowledge. Everybody knows that," he replied. He then went on to spend the rest of the evening telling me about the vicious in-fighting within the spiritual organization.

"Sound like some of the key players are eating meat," I said.

"Oh, no. They're too spiritual for that," he said.

Christianity/Metaphysical Merger

Q.

Maybe I'm reading between the lines, but it seems to me that you don't think there is any possibility of a merger between Christianity and metaphysics?

A.

Some organizations, such as the A.R.E. (Association For Research & Enlightenment), have never seen any contradictions between the two, but I contend they simply choose to ignore the irreconcilable differences. The basis of all Eastern thought is "We are all one—we are part of God, thus we are also God." Christianity must separate "Father, Son and Holy Ghost." Metaphysics says, "Go inside and find your own answers." Christianity says, "We have the answers and if you don't adhere to them, you'll go to hell." The concept of a devil and damnation have always been the Christian priest-craft's device to control followers. How can you possibly fit that into a loving metaphysical system of self-responsibility? Metaphysics and Paganism never try to convert. Christianity has a bloody history of Inquisitions, coercion and wars fought to force its beliefs upon the masses. Today, if the Pope or Religious Right had the power, they would force everyone by law to accept their Dark-Age thinking.

Hopefully, metaphysics will prove to be the enlightened spiritual system which will follow Christianity and other fear-based religions that are now losing followers at an ever-increasing rate. People are tired of being fleeced and fed fairy tales.

Q&A

I received ninety-six letters in response to the above answer. Many of the letters said, "Thanks for pointing it out." But at least fifty of the responses were from people who were quite upset with me for not thinking as they do. Some of the communications were intelligent, but most were from those lacking the ability to distinguish their desires from reality. It is this inability to distinguish up from down, valid from hoax, logic from foo-foo, that causes the media to label the New Age a joke.

A few nice letters were from Unity members. I personally like Unity, but to traditional Christian churches, Unity is a cult. Unity links Christianity with metaphysical principals, but that is not merging Christianity and metaphysics. Christianity is not the teachings of Jesus. Christianity is a group of self-serving religious institutions that have distorted the original teaching beyond recognition.

Many Christian denominations have recently ripped themselves apart over such subjects as female priests and acknowledging homosexuals. Now, relate that to REALITY and imagine an ecumenical council in which the head priest says, "Well, it's time we merged with metaphysics. So now we'll give up the idea of hell. We'll accept reincarnation and karma again. We'll drop the birth-control thing. And, oh yeah, the Father, Son and Holy Ghost bit doesn't relate anymore."

And if you think that's going to happen, I'm selling five-pound gold bricks for $9.98. Metaphysics is an awareness for the next century. It isn't a religion and it will never merge with Christianity. I hope the pure teachings of Jesus are taught forever, along with the teachings of Buddha, Krishna, Lao Tsu, Chuang Tsu, and the many other great spiritual communicators.

Q.

You seem to forget that the United States of America is a Christian country, Mr. Sutphen.

A.

Nothing could be further from the truth. Let me begin my response by quoting **George Washington:** "The United States is in no sense founded upon the Christian religion."

Take out a dollar bill and observe Washington on the front and occult symbology on the back. The founding fathers of our nation were Masons, members of a metaphysical awareness structure known as Freemasonry. Fifty of the fifty-six men who signed the Declaration of Independence were Masons. Four of the five members of the Constitutional Convention were Master Masons—which means master metaphysicians.

The restrictive theology of Christianity could never have resulted in the freedom of the Bill of Rights and the Constitution. The Bill of Rights contains tenets from the Masonic Order. Even the date, July 4, 1776, was charted astrologically. When George Washington, in full Masonic regalia, laid the cornerstone of the White House, he incorporated a 6,000-year-old Egyptian ritual.

The United States was founded upon occultism, and it is those metaphysical freedoms that have carried us this far.

The following quote was made by **Thomas Jefferson** to Dr. Benjamin Rush, September 23, 1800. (The original in the Library of Congress shows "god" spelled with a small "g.") "They (the clergy) believe that any portion of power confided to me will be exerted in opposition to their schemes. And they believe right, for I have sworn upon the altar of god, eternal hostility against every form of tyranny over the mind of man."

Bhagwan Shree Rajneesh

Q.

Many followers of Bhagwan Shree Rajneesh have written to me—some upset by my views, others thanking me for acknowledging their guru. In contrast to much of my mail, all the communications have been respectful and intelligent. An 11-page letter arrived from Swami Devageet (Charles Newman), a 50-year-old dental surgeon in Poona, India. Swami Anand Bodhicitta (Andrew Ferber), a 52-year-old Professor of Psychiatry at Albert Einstein College of Medicine in Bronx, New York, sent four pages.

Both men argue with my position on meditation, and both refer to my tape, *The Battle For Your Mind* (a talk given at the World Congress of Professional Hypnotists Convention, which is basically covered in the Brainwashing chapter in this book), and previous communications in this column. Both asked questions representative of the rest of my mail and both invited me to come to India to experience Bhagwan directly.

The other side of the coin was the irrational mail I received from people who hate everything about Rajneesh and who condemned me for saying, "If Bhagwan were judged solely upon his discourses, he is the wisest of all."

A.

In response to many questions: Do I think Bhagwan Shree Rajneesh is an enlightened Master? I don't know. Do I think I am a Master? No. I want to make that very clear. I know enlightenment, as commonly perceived, doesn't exist. I'm a writer and a seminar trainer ... a "way clearer," as I've said many times. To those asking, "Why don't you read Bhagwan's books?" I reply, "I have read at least 30—all transcribed discourses. I've also listened to his tapes and I receive the *Rajneesh Times.*"

You are correct in accusing me of having no direct experience of Bhagwan. He hasn't had the direct experience of many he has challenged. My words about his losing the ability to "live his teachings for awhile" are based on the words and writings of others. But this is not a criticism.

Even a Master is not a superman, always wise in the ways of the world, nor should he be expected to be. He exists on the manifest plane to share awareness that transcends the world. Jesus wasn't too wise in damning the fig tree for not feeding him when it was the wrong season for figs. Bhagwan hasn't always been wise in dealing with the world. Granted, no one—including a Master—should have to deal with the likes of the FBI, CIA, or right-wing politicians.

You argue, "Antelope, Oregon, was part of the lesson." There is no way to disagree, but that argument works both ways and can be used to rationalize almost anything. Let's just say Bhagwan's teachings encompass some of the best of Buddha and Lao Tsu. Then would it not be accurate to say Rajneesh wasn't living his teachings when his organization responded with militancy in Oregon? But so what? Karmically, it **was** part of the lesson—for Bhagwan, as well as everyone else. And, as I was quick to point out, "that doesn't diminish the value of his teachings."

In regard to people being hurt: From an earthly perspective, that is certainly true. There are plenty of followers who have exhibited the classic symptoms of conversion (brainwashing) withdrawal. I see this as their karma and part of their lesson. Bhagwan helped them experience exactly what they needed to experience. Does that excuse Bhagwan? I don't know. Karma gets tricky and I'm in no position to judge anything but the fact that some people were hurt.

In my seminar, a woman gains enough self-awareness to walk away from a bad marriage. Did I cause the divorce? Several fundamentalist Christian anti-New Age books list me as a devil incarnate. Am I?

Obviously, we are not about to agree on the issue of excessive meditation. I view the effect as undesirable. You see the same effect as beneficial. We also will not agree on the need of a guru. But no matter what path each of us walks, I have no doubt we will all eventually evolve to the same level of awareness.

You are mistaken in thinking I am against Bhagwan. His words always make me think and he has influenced my communications in many ways. I find him one of the few refreshing, grounded voices in a wilderness of cosmic foo-foos. Bhagwan has asked the press to "write lies about me, for that is the only way you will get my name into print." How sad, because this radical East Indian has so much to say that the world needs to hear. Obviously, articles about miracle courses or a woman who channels "Muga from Mars" are less threatening to the establishment.

The Harmonic Convergence

Q.

Are you going to tell your readers that the Harmonic Convergence II (July 26, 1992) is just New Age baloney? It would be better for all of us if we can find harmony in this. The Harmonic Convergence was the only thing that has brought the metaphysical community together on such a large scale.

A.

As I expressed in 1987, to me, the Harmonic Convergence was the biggest New Age embarrassment of the century. Does everyone reading this know that on that date (August 16/17, 1987) the fate of the planet hung in the balance? Just like you, I'm sure glad thousands of New Agers met at the sacred sites around the world to meditate and save us.

After that date, we entered a new cycle and everything was

supposed to get better. Personally, I haven't noticed much difference in the world. The recession that started in 1990 wasn't better. The Gulf War sucked. And all the other wars and conflicts since 1987 feel like business as usual.

According to *The Mayan Factor* by Jose Arguelles—the book that started it all—the ancient Mayans were aliens from the Galactic Federation who left the earth in luminous cocoons in 800 A.D. They did, however, leave their calendar for Arguelles to decipher, which he did, and he decided the Mayans were coming back in 1992. This was supposed to result in our forsaking our rationalist ways to tune into the Galactic Mind.

In a "Magical Blend" magazine interview, Arguelles said, "By the summer of 1992 the resistance of the collapsing old mental house will pretty much come to an end." He goes on to explain that within this new 20-year phase, "...we're going to be given the opportunity to relax and let a final flowering occur. By 2012 when the cycle closes out, that's when we shift to evolutionary patterns and that's when we get completely interfaced with what I call the Galactic Federation."

Okay, Jose. Even if it doesn't go down like that, I like the counterpoint to the soothsayers predicting doomsday in the following chapter.

Smoke And Mirrors

Q.

Why do you use your column to expose things you don't agree with? It's not very spiritual.

A.

The repeating message in my "Controversial Questions" column is, *being a true believer doesn't work!* Stop accepting ungrounded spiritual and human-potential concepts that do not serve you. Separate wishful thinking from reality. Take the effort to see through the smoke and mirrors. Get real. Wake up. If you see this as "exposing things I don't agree with," that's what you got out of it.

CHAPTER 11

THE END TIMES

etween the riots, crime, fires and earthquakes, an over-zealous media has fostered an Armageddon **image** of Southern California. I don't want to sound like the Los Angeles Chamber of Commerce, but this **image** isn't what is. The weather is balmy, the atmosphere peaceful. The people here are generally warm and friendly, their attitude nonjudgmental and laid-back. There are more spiritual offerings and activities per capita than anywhere in the country. The Agoura Hills area, where we have our offices, has the second lowest crime rate in the 13 western states and nearby Simi Valley is the lowest in the nation. Statistically, even the City of Los Angeles has lower crime than most major western cities.

A large percentage of the nation's metaphysical authors and psychics reside here. None I'm aware of accept the idea of earth changes or foresee the "big one" in the near future. The January earthquake killed 55 people, but to put that figure in perspective, the average L.A. death toll during that time was greatly reduced. In other words, because the city came to a standstill, more people are alive today because of the quake than would have been if it had not occurred. Also, during the same two week period, 150 people died in the Eastern winter storm.

Images are the most powerful form of communication. That's why politicians use them to get elected, advertisers to sell products, and the news media to hype ratings. But too often the **images** are inaccurate manipulations.

While researching my book, *The Mad Old Ads* (McGraw Hill, 1967), I learned how effectively public opinion was manipulated by stage plays in 19th Century England. Today, TV news and movie images program the viewer. Most movie viewers don't stop to realize that any violent L.A. images would be just as appropriate in their own city.

In my books and seminars, I've often said, "I am whatever you think I am. How could I be anything else?" Your perceptions become what is for you. From a human-potential perspective, seeing through misleading images is a key part of expanding awareness.

If you don't live in Southern California, your image of the area isn't important in the wide range of human events. But perceiving an accurate image of the people and events that directly affect your life is very important. We're all served by looking beneath surface impressions and by taking TV sound bites, movie images and the predictions of soothsayers with a grain of salt.   **—Editorial, June 1994**

Q.

"How can you remain in California when Nostradamus has predicted the end of California on May 10th?" (Many letters asked this question.) "... *Earthwatch* just might be correct in predicting that the early morning hour of May 23, 1988 will see the start of the earthquake action." (Earthwatch/ META Science Foundation: God and Science Working Together) "Don't you realize that Ramtha has told everyone to leave California because the end times are coming!" (Many letters asked this question, also.)

A.

The month of May has come and gone, and once again the New Age community has been made to look like (the) fools (that many are). The *Los Angeles Times* and "Doonesbury" had a field day with the thousands who panicked or left town during the May dates in question. They hadn't had so much fun since the harmonic convergence.

California has always had earthquakes, and always will, but please do not credit the next one to Nostradamus. Those who have loosely interpreted the 16th-century seer are the ones who have retroactively made him accurate about historical predications. I had never heard of META-science until they sent me their large packet of scare propaganda titled, "Collapse & Comeback." (They report getting pictures of dead people on a broken TV set, which must explain "God and science working together.")

Until we grow up and stop buying into every cosmic foo-foo convergence/prediction/idea that comes along, only the metaphysically "disabled" are going to take New Age ideas seriously. We are our own worst enemies and we scare off many responsible people who might otherwise begin to embrace our concepts.

Q.

Do you and Tara agree with Ruth Montgomery's guides, Edgar Cayce, and others, that the earth will shift on its axis around the year 2000, resulting in the death of millions?

A.

No. Invariably, psychic and religious predictors set dates for an apocalypse—the world was supposed to end at least six times in the first five years. When it doesn't happen, they set a new date. True believers, seeming unmoved by logic or rational thinking, accept the next date, because it's what they subconsciously desire.

I love Ruth Montgomery personally and we've worked together in the past, but both her guides and Cayce's source have been wrong.

Q&A

Judging by mail volume, the most controversial question in 1993 was in regard to Los Angeles experiencing "the Big One" and "falling into the sea." A big-name earthquake predictor and several psychics set a day in May. Nostradamus was said to have predicted the same fate would occur in June.

My son Scott said that people called him at his Malibu Shaman store weeks prior to these predicted events, panicked over the two dates. And he couldn't keep the latest Nostradamus book in stock.

During the spring, every metaphysical true believer I talked to wanted to know if I was leaving California.

"I don't accept the predictions," I said, and neither do any of the psychics I know." They were shocked.

Tara and I were autographing books in a West Hollywood store shortly after the May date came and went without incident. A young woman asked if we were leaving town before the June date.

"Nothing happened in May," I said.

"Oh, that's because a hundred of us got together and prayed to save the state," she said. All sincerity.

"Save us again in June, okay?"

The *Los Angeles Times* recently ran an article about all the incorrect doomsday predictions, from born-again Christian Hal Lindsey's *The Late Great Planet Earth* date for Armageddon to the latest New Age offerings. It was a long article, covering a lot of predictions—none accurate.

If you're going to worry about prophecies you can do nothing about, why not try to focus the same energy upon something real you can do plenty about, such as improving a relationship, or helping someone in need? To me, if it's your karma to experience a catastrophe, you will. You might escape California only to move to Iowa and die in a flood.

Q.

As I see it, we need a pole shift to purge the earth, which, as a sentient entity, is reacting to our terrible treatment of it. Our world population is 5.5 billion and we are using up the earth's resources at an irreplaceable rate. Can you imagine the present population nearly doubled and all the resources gone? Those making this prediction believe the earth's population will be decimated so that something will be left to sustain the more highly evolved. A place will be found on other planets for those who lost their lives in this predicted purging—a place where they can further evolve.

A.

It sounds like you're arguing for the end of the world as if it were something to be voted on. Maybe you need this cleansing as a way to purge your blighted life. I'm not saying this is so, but it's a valid question for anyone preoccupied with the "end times."

Assuming the poles don't shift, which scientists don't accept as an imminent threat, let's look at the idea of using up our resources: Thomas Malthus predicted the growth of population would outstrip the world's food supply during the 19th century. Wrong.

In nearly all fields of human endeavor, technology has found ways to use resources without exhausting them. As an example, because of new economizing technology, oil consumption continues to go down. In the last decade, it fell 9.3 percent in the U.S. and Canada and 15.8 percent in Europe—in spite of economic and population growth. Many worried that our telecommunications needs would use up all the copper, but today fiber optics cable (made of silica sand) carries a thousand times more messages than a copper wire. A ton of copper is now replaced by a cable made from only 25 kilograms of sand, which can be produced with only five percent of the energy needed to produce the copper wire it replaces.

Your computer-like mind manifests your personal reality as a reflection of your inner thoughts. That being the case, doesn't it make more sense to believe that technology will save us? What's the alternative? Get depressed? Become a condom activist? Promote the selective elimination of an undesirable segment of the population?

Expect incredible advances in science, food technology, nutrition and medicine; solar power, anti-gravity, flight, high-tech homes costing a fraction of today's models, and simple birth control for developing nations. I believe it.

Q.

In response to my story about the Malibu firestorms, I received many letters like these, arguing for more devastation:

"You say we have always had natural disasters which is true but not so many so close together. When the 'big one' strikes California, your part west of the San Andreas fault may break off and fall into the Pacific Ocean.

"I feel you are quite blase about the devastation in your area. Do you really believe that the psychics who predict much more devastation are listening to false, uniformed voices? Are yours the only valid ones? Many say that the fires are a warning to people to leave before things get worse."

A.

According to all the geologists, the state can quake, but cannot "fall into" the Ocean. If the poles shift, the entire planet would experience transition, and I wouldn't want to count on Montana being safe, even if Edgar Cayce says so. If you live in fear of a pole shift, I feel sorry for you.

Who are the many who say? I haven't heard one responsible person with a published psychic track record say anything like that. And where would you have people go? When I lived in

Minneapolis, many a night we slept in the basement because of tornado warnings. In Scottsdale, Arizona, a tornado wiped out several houses one street away from mine. How about floods in Iowa, hurricanes in Florida, blizzards in the Northeast? A lady from Arkansas recently told me about her problems with poisonous snakes.

In his book *The True Believer,* Eric Hoffer talks about those who gleefully anticipate the millennium: "They see in a general downfall an approach to the brotherhood of all. Chaos, like the grave, is a haven of equality. Their burning conviction that there must be a new life and a new order is fueled by the realization that the old will have to be razed to the ground before the new can be built. Their clamor for a millennium is shot through with a hatred for all that exists, and a craving for the end of the world."

Jess Stearn recently came to our house for dinner, and we discussed this subject for probably the hundredth time. To sum it up, he said, "Don't worry about where you live, but *how* you live."

Q&A

Remember the U.S. map with Nebraska as a seacoast? It was popularized by the 1978 book, *We Are The Earthquake Generation* by Jeffrey Goodman? I've met thousands of people who took it seriously. According to Goodman between 1980 and 1985, Palm Springs was supposed to be submerged. San Diego, Los Angeles and San Francisco were supposed to be destroyed. The California coastline was supposed to be pushed back to Bakersfield and Sacramento. Also predicted: The destruction of part of New York City, a new land bridge between Siberia and Alaska, and a seaway opening from Oregon to Idaho.

Between 1985 and 1990 New York was supposed to be destroyed, and the earth's axis of rotation was supposed to tip a few degrees. Now it's really time to worry, because according to Goodman, between 1990 and 2000, Nebraska will become the western coastline, Jesus will return with lots of helpers, and space people will visit and observe.

Q.

Your lack of respect for Edgar Cayce is disgraceful.

A.

I have considerable respect for much that Cayce communicated, including medical advice that has helped me personally. But Cayce wasn't infallible. While his medical information was quite accurate, his earth-change predictions were not. Cayce said Atlantis would rise again in '68 or '69. In 1941 he predicted that New York would disappear within another generation. "Much sooner than this," he said, the southern portions of Carolina and Georgia would disappear.

I feel part of Cayce's channeling sourced subconscious memories of an incarnation as a medical practitioner in a holistically advanced, past civilization.

Q&A

The Millennium Thing: I have no intention of continuing to argue *against* the end of the world ... or the end of California.

As a parting report on this foo-foo hysteria: During one week in June 1994, after someone reported the appearance of an angel in the back seat of their car, people all over Southern California started reporting angels in their cars, causing them to momentarily lose control of their vehicles. When CHP officers pulled over the erratic drivers they heard this excuse: "An angel appeared and told me to leave town because there's going to be a terrible earthquake this weekend." Because so many drivers gave the same excuse, the story made the local papers, resulting in more incidents. For days, panicked people called the Malibu Shaman, asking Scott if it was true. New Agers left the city. AND ... the weekend came and went without incident.

CHAPTER 12

CULTS, RELIGIONS & BRAINWASHING

Q.

You are against the idea of a New Age Movement becoming a real movement. Why?

A.

A movement made up of people searching within could change the planet. But a literal New Age Movement is incompatible with everything we stand for. For starters, "true believers" form the bulk of all movements and causes, and by joining an organization, they fulfill their own dysfunctional needs:

1) Faith in their cause replaces their lost faith themselves. 2) The less self-esteem someone has, the more likely they are to identify with a cause. 3) A cause allows its followers to renounce an unwanted, unworthy self and experience rebirth through identification with the worthwhile efforts of the quest.

Q.

According to your criteria, anyone who has attended an est seminar, experienced U.S. Army boot camp, been saved in a Christian crusade, or joined the Hare Krishnas has been brainwashed. That list includes me and I am not brainwashed.

A.

In the entire history of man, no one has ever been brainwashed and realized, or believed, that he was brainwashed. Those who have been brainwashed will usually passionately defend their manipulators, claiming they have simply been "shown the light," or experienced a miraculous transformation.

Q.

You often talk about conversion and brainwashing being used by religions. I know some pretty crazy religious people, but I don't think they're brainwashed.

A.

Conversion is a nice word for **brainwashing,** and any study of brainwashing has to begin with a study of Christian revivalism in eighteenth century America. Jonathan Edwards accidently discovered the techniques during a religious crusade in 1735 in Northampton, Massachusetts. By inducing guilt and acute apprehension and by increasing the tension, the "sinners" attending his revival meetings would break down and completely submit. Technically, Edwards was creating conditions that wiped the brain slate clean so his listeners would accept new programming, but in this case new negative programming. He told them, "You're sinners, destined for hell!" As a result, many went into terrible depression. One person committed suicide and another attempted suicide. The neighbors of the suicidal converts related that they, too, were affected so deeply that, although they had found "eternal salvation," they were obsessed with a diabolical temptation to end their own lives.

Once a preacher, cult leader, manipulator or authority figure creates a brain phase to wipe the brain-slate clean, his subjects will accept new suggestions, which can be substituted for their previous ideas. Because Edwards didn't turn his message positive until the end of the crusade, many accepted the negative suggestions and acted, or desired to act, upon them.

Charles J. Finney was another Christian revivalist who used the same techniques four years later in mass-religious conversions in New York. The techniques are still being used today by Christians, cults, human-potential trainings, some business rallies, and the U.S. Armed Services.

Q.

What are the brain phases that can cause you to be so suggestible?

A.

The Christians may have been the first to successfully formulate brainwashing, but we have to look to Ivan Petravich Pavlov, the Russian scientist, for a technical explanation. In the early 1900s, his work with animals opened the door to further investigations with humans. After the revolution in Russia, Lenin was quick to see the potential of applying Pavlov's research to his own ends.

Three distinct and progressive states of transmarginal inhibition were identified by Pavlov. The first is the **Equivalent** phase, in which the brain gives the same response to both strong and weak stimuli. The second is the **Paradoxical** phase, in which the brain responds more actively to weak stimuli than to strong. Third is the **Ultra-Paradoxical** phase, in which conditioned responses and behavior patterns turn from positive to negative or from negative to positive.

With the progression through each phase, the degree of conversion becomes more effective and complete. The ways to achieve conversion are many and varied, but the usual first step in religious or political brainwashing is to work on the emotions of an individual or group until they reach an abnormal level of anger, fear, excitement or nervous tension.

The progressive result of this mental condition is to impair judgment and increase suggestibility. The more this condition can be maintained or intensified, the more it compounds. Once catharsis is reached, the complete mental takeover becomes easier. Existing mental programming can be replaced with new patterns of thinking and behavior.

Other often-used physiological weapons to modify normal brain functions are fasting, radical or high sugar diets, physical discomforts, regulation of breathing, mantra chanting, the disclosure of awesome mysteries, special lighting and sound effects/music, programmed response to incense, or intoxicating drugs.

The same results can be obtained in contemporary psychiatric treatment by electric shock treatments or even by purposely lowering a patient's blood sugar level with insulin injections.

Q.

What do revivalist-style preachers do to convert people attending their crusades?

A.

For a real education, check this out for yourself at a local fundamentalist church, or the next time a crusade comes to your area. Go to the church or tent early and sit in the rear. Most likely, repetitive music will be played while the people come in for the service. A repetitive beat, ideally ranging from 45 to 72 beats per minute (a rhythm close to the beat of a human heart), is very hypnotic and can generate an eyes-open altered state of consciousness in a high percentage of people. And, once you are in an alpha state, you are at least 25 times as suggestible as you would be in full beta consciousness. The music is probably the same for every service, or incorporates the same beat, and many of the people will go into an altered state soon after entering the sanctuary. Subconsciously, they recall their state of mind from previous services and respond according to the post-hypnotic programming.

Watch the people waiting for the service to begin. Many will exhibit external signs of trance—body relaxation and dilated eyes. Often, they begin swaying back and forth with their hands in the air while sitting in their chairs.

Next, the assistant pastor will probably come out and speak with a "voice roll"—a patterned, paced verbal style used by hypnotists when inducing a trance. It is also used by many lawyers, several of whom are highly trained hypnotists, when they desire to entrench a point firmly in the minds of the jurors. A voice roll can sound as if the speaker were talking to the beat of a metronome or it may sound as though he were emphasizing every word in a monotonous, patterned style. The words will usually be delivered at the rate of 45 to 60 beats per minute, maximizing the hypnotic effect.

Now the assistant pastor begins the "build-up" process. He induces an altered state of consciousness and/or begins to generate the excitement and the expectations of the audience. Next, a group of young women in "sweet and pure" chiffon dresses might come out to sing a song. Gospel songs are great for building excitement and involvement. In the middle of the song, one of the girls might be "smitten" and fall down or react as if possessed by the Holy Spirit. This effectively increases the intensity in the room. At this point, hypnosis and conversion tactics are being mixed, and the audience's attention is now focused upon the communications while the environment becomes more exciting and tense.

About this time, when an eyes-open mass-induced alpha mental state has been achieved, they will usually pass the collection plate or basket. In the background, a 45-beat-per-minute voice roll from the assistant preacher might exhort, "Give to God ... Give to God ... Give to God ..." And the audience gives. God may not get the money, but his already wealthy representative will.

Next, the headliner—the fire-and-brimstone preacher comes out. He induces fear and increases the tension by talking about the devil, going to hell, or the forthcoming Armageddon.

In the last such rally I attended, the preacher talked about blood that would soon be running out of every faucet in the land. He was also obsessed with a "bloody axe of God," which his congregation has seen hanging above the pulpit the previous week. I have no doubt that many saw it—the power of suggestion given to hundreds of people in hypnosis assures that at least 10 to 25 percent would see whatever the preacher suggested they see.

In most revivalist gatherings, "testifying" or "witnessing" usually follows the fear-based sermon. People from the audience come up on stage and relate their stories. "I was crippled and now I can walk!" "I had arthritis and now it's gone!" It is a psychological manipulation that works. After listening to numerous case histories of miraculous healings, the average attendee with a minor problem is sure he/she can be healed. The room is charged with fear, guilt, intense excitement and expectations.

Those who want to be healed are often lined up around the edge of the room, or they are told to come down to the front. The preacher might touch them on the head and scream, "Be healed!" This releases the psychic energy and tosses many into catharsis—a purging of repressed emotions. Individuals often cry hysterically, fall down or go into spasms. And if catharsis is effected, they stand a chance of being healed. In catharsis, the brain-slate is temporarily wiped clean and new suggestions will be accepted.

For some, the healing may be permanent. For many it will last four days to a week—which is, incidentally, how long a hypnotic suggestion given to a somnambulistic subject usually lasts. Even if the healing doesn't last, if the true believer comes back every week the power of suggestion may continually override or mask the physical problem.

I'm not saying that legitimate healings do not take place. They do. Maybe the individual is ready to let go of the negativity causing the problem, or maybe the healing is the work of God. But more often than not, on-the-spot, miraculous healings can be explained by brain/mind function.

The techniques and staging will vary from church to church. Many use "speaking in tongues" to generate catharsis in some while the spectacle creates intense excitement in the others.

The use of hypnotic and conversion techniques by religions is sophisticated, and professionals are assuring they become even more effective. A man in Los Angeles is designing, building and reworking churches around the country. He tells ministers what they need and how to use the most effective techniques of conversion. This man's track record indicates that the size of a congregation and the monetary income will double if the minister follows his instructions. He admits that about 80 percent of his efforts are in the sound system and lighting.

Powerful sound and the proper use of lighting are of primary importance in inducing an altered state of consciousness. I've been using them for years in my own seminars. However, my participants are fully aware of the process and what they can expect as a result of participation.

Q.

I don't want to be brainwashed. What do I look out for when attending activities sponsored by spiritual organizations?

A.

Cults, religions and human-potential organizations are always looking for new converts. To attain them, many create a brain-phase. And they often need to do it within a short space of time—a weekend, a day, and in some cases a one-evening orientation.

The meeting or training takes place in an area where participants are cut off from the outside world. This may be any place: a private home, a remote or rural setting, or even a hotel ballroom where the participants are allowed only limited bathroom usage. In human-potential trainings, the controllers will give a lengthy talk about the importance of "keeping agreements" in life. The participants are told that if they don't keep agreements, their life will never work. It's a good idea to keep agreements, but the controllers are subverting a positive human value for selfish purposes. The participants vow to themselves and their trainer that they will keep their agreements. Anyone who does not will be intimidated into agreement or forced to leave. The next step is to agree to complete the training, thus assuring a high percentage of conversions for the organization. They will usually have to agree not to take drugs or smoke and sometimes not to eat ... or they are given such a short meal break that it creates tension. The real reason for the agreements is to alter internal chemistry, which generates anxiety and hopefully causes at least a slight malfunction of the nervous system, which in turn increases the conversion potential.

Before the gathering is complete, the agreements will be used to ensure that the new converts go out and find new participants. They are intimidated into agreeing to do so before they leave. Since the importance of keeping agreements is so high on their priority list, the converts will twist the arms of everyone they know, attempting to talk them into attending a free introductory session offered at a future date by the organization. The new converts are zealots. In fact, the inside term for merchandising human-potential trainings is, "sell it by zealot!"

Well over a million people are human-potential-training graduates, and a good percentage have been left with a mental activation button that assures their future loyalty and assistance if the guru figure or organization calls. Think about the potential political implications of hundreds of thousands of zealots programmed to campaign for their guru or preacher, or the candidate of their guru or preacher.

Be wary of an organization of this type that offers follow-up sessions after a seminar. Follow-up sessions might be weekly meetings or inexpensive seminars given on a regular basis which the organization will attempt to talk you into taking—or any regularly scheduled event used to maintain control. As the early Christian revivalists found, long-term control is dependent upon a good follow-up system.

The second conversion indicator: A schedule is maintained that causes physical and mental fatigue. This is primarily accomplished by long hours in which the participants are given no opportunity for relaxation or reflection.

The third conversion indicator: Techniques are used to increase the tension in the room or environment.

The fourth indicator is uncertainty. The participants become concerned about being "put on the spot" by the trainers, who play upon guilt feelings and encourage participants to relate their innermost secrets to the other participants. In some situations the trainer forces activities that emphasize the removal of masks. One of the most successful human-potential seminars forces the participants to stand on a stage in front of the entire audience while being verbally attacked by the trainers. According to public opinion polls, to speak in front of an audience is the most fearful possible situation. It ranked above window washing outside the 85th floor of an office building. So you can imagine the fear and tension this situation generates within the participants. Many faint, but most cope with the stress by mentally "going away." They literally go into an alpha state, which automatically makes them many times as suggestible as they normally are. And another loop of the downward spiral into conversion is successfully effected.

The fifth clue that conversion tactics are being used is the introduction of jargon—new terms that have meaning only to the "insiders" who participate. Vicious language is also frequently used, purposely, to make participants uncomfortable.

The final tip-off is that there is no humor in the communications, at least until the participants are converted. Then, merrymaking and humor are highly desirable as symbols of the new joy the participants have supposedly found.

I'm not saying that good does not result from participation in such gatherings. Many are served. But I contend it is important for people to know what has happened and to be aware that continual involvement may not be in their best interest.

Over the years, I've conducted professional seminars to teach people to be hypnotists, trainers and counselors. I've had many of those who conduct trainings and rallies come to me and say, "I'm here because I know what I'm doing works, but I don't know why." After showing them how and why, many have gotten out of the business or have decided to approach it differently or in a much more loving and supportive manner.

Many of these trainers have become personal friends, and it scares us all to have experienced the power of one person with a microphone and a room full of people. Add a little charisma and you can count on a high percentage of conversion. The sad truth is that a high percentage of people want to give away their power—they are "true believers."

Cult gatherings or human-potential trainings are an ideal environment to observe first-hand what is technically called the "Stockholm Syndrome." This is a situation in which those who are intimidated, controlled or made to suffer, begin to love, admire and even sometimes sexually desire their controllers or captors.

Let me inject a word of warning here: If you think you can attend such gatherings and not be affected, you are probably wrong. A perfect example is the case of a woman who went to Haiti on a Guggenheim Fellowship to study Haitian Voodoo. In her report, she related how the music eventually induced uncontrollable bodily movement and an altered state of consciousness. Although she understood the process and thought herself above it, when she began to feel herself become vulnerable to the music, she attempted to fight it and turned away. Anger or resistance almost always assures conversion. A few moments later she was possessed by the music and began dancing in a trance around the Voodoo meeting house. A brain phase had been induced by the music and excitement, and she awoke feeling reborn. The only hope of attending such gatherings without being affected is to be the Buddha and allow no positive or negative emotions to surface. Few people are capable of such detachment.

Before I go on, let's go back to the six tip-offs to conversion. I want to mention the United States Government and military boot camp. The Marine Corps talks about breaking men down before "rebuilding" them as new men—as marines! Well, that is exactly what they do, the same way a cult breaks its people down and rebuilds them as happy flower sellers on your local street corner. Every one of the six conversion techniques are used in boot camp. Considering the needs of the military, I'm not making a judgment as to whether this is good or bad, but the soldiers are effectively brainwashed.

Decognition Process

Once the initial conversion is effected, cults, armed services and similar groups cannot have cynicism among their members. Members must respond to commands and do as they are told, otherwise, they are dangerous to the organization. This control is normally accomplished as a three-step Decognition Process.

Step one is **Alertness Reduction:** The controllers cause the nervous system to malfunction, making it difficult to distinguish between fantasy and reality. This can be accomplished in several ways. **Poor diet** is one; watch out for brownies and Koolaid. The sugar throws the nervous system off. More subtle is the **"spiritual diet"** used by many cults. They eat only vegetables and fruits; without the grounding of grains, nuts, seeds, dairy products, fish or meat, an individual becomes mentally "spacey." **Inadequate sleep** is another way to reduce alertness, especially when combined with long hours of work or intense physical activity. Being bombarded with intense and unique experiences achieves the same result.

Step two is **Programmed Confusion:** You are mentally assaulted while your alertness is being reduced as in Step One. This is accomplished with a deluge of new information, lectures, discussion groups, encounters or one-to-one processing, which usually amounts to the controller bombarding the individual with questions. During this phase of decognition, reality and illusion often merge and perverted logic is likely to be accepted.

Step three is **Thought Stopping:** Techniques are used to cause the mind to go "flat." These are altered-state-of-consciousness techniques that initially induce calmness by giving the mind something simple to deal with and focusing awareness. The continued use brings on a feeling of elation and eventually hallucination. The result is the reduction of thought and eventually, if used long enough, the cessation of all thought and withdrawal from everyone and everything except that which the controllers direct. The takeover is then complete. It is important to be aware that when members or participants are instructed to use "thought-stopping" techniques they are told that they will benefit by so doing; they will become "better soldiers" or "find peace," or "attain enlightenment."

There are three primary techniques used for thought stopping. The first is **Marching**. The thump, thump, thump beat literally generates an altered state of consciousness and thus great susceptibility to suggestions. Adolf Hitler used marching demonstrations and excitement as a mass-conversion technique in the primary phase for those attending his rallies, and in the decognition phase for his soldiers. The observers, entranced by the activity, were opened to accepting his suggestions.

The second thought-stopping technique is **Meditation.** If you spend 90 minutes to two hours a day in meditation, after a few weeks, you probably won't return to full beta consciousness, as long as you continue to meditate. I'm not saying this is bad. If you do it yourself, it may be very beneficial. But it is a fact that you are mellowing out by mentally detaching. But you detach right across the board, from the good as well as the bad, very much as you would do if smoking grass or taking Valium.

I've worked with meditators on an EEG machine and the results are conclusive: the more hours per day you meditate, the flatter your mind becomes. When extensive meditation is combined with a "spiritual" diet (strict vegetarian without proper protein balance) and decognition, all true independent thought will eventually cease. Some spiritual groups see this as nirvana, but it is simply a predictable physiological result. I doubt that heaven on earth amounts to non-thinking and non-involvement.

The third thought-stopping technique is **Chanting**, and often chanting in meditation. "Speaking in tongues" could also be included in this category.

All three thought-stopping techniques produce an altered state of consciousness, which in turn releases endorphins—a brain/mind opiate that is chemically nearly identical to opium. Meditators feel "good," "spiritual," "high on harmony." Distance runners automatically go into an altered state they call a "runner's high." Writers sit uninterrupted for hours at a computer keyboard, and many claim to "disappear" and let the story write itself. Researchers claim you're in an altered state two-thirds of the time you're watching television.

Endorphins explain why each activity is so enjoyable and why it is addictive. Such altered states are predictable and measurable and the resulting **detachment** is predictable. If you're in alpha more than 90 minutes a day, this may or may not serve you. You may not be as easily agitated by outside conditions, but you also may lose some interest in enriching day-to-day activities.

True Believers & Mass Movements

Based upon my experience in working with people, I'm convinced that approximately one third of the population is what

Eric Hoffer calls "true believers." They are joiners and followers ... people who want to give away their power. They look for answers, meaning and enlightenment outside themselves in mass movements: cults, religions and causes (political, environmental, et cetera).

Hoffer's book, *The True Believer*, is a classic on mass movement. He says, "True believers are not intent on bolstering and advancing a cherished self, but are those craving to be rid of an unwanted self. They are followers, not because of a desire for self-advancement, but because it can satisfy their passion for self-renunciation!" Hoffer also says that true believers "are eternally incomplete and eternally insecure."

In my workshops and seminars, I come in contact with many true believers. All I can do is attempt to show them that answers lie within. I communicate that the basics of spirituality are self-responsibility and self-actualization. But most of these seekers tell me that I'm not spiritual and go looking for someone who will give them the dogma and structure they desire.

Never underestimate the potential danger of these people. They can easily be molded into fanatics who will gladly work and die for their holy cause, which is a substitute for their lost faith in themselves. The cause usually offers them a substitute for individual hope. They are fanatics who believe they hold the one-and-only answer.

Mass movements have charismatic leaders. The followers are obsessed with converting others to their way of living or impose a new way of life—if necessary, by legislating laws forcing others to their view, as evidenced by the activities of the Religious Right. In the end, all laws mean enforcement by police and punishment for refusing to comply.

A common hatred, enemy or devil is essential to the success of a mass movement. Hitler's devil was the Jews; the Born-Again Christians have Satan himself, but that isn't enough—they've added, homosexuals, pro-choice women, the New Age, civil libertarians, humanists, and all who oppose their integration of church and state. In revolutions, the "devil" is usually the ruling power or aristocracy. Some human-potential movements are far too clever to ask their graduates to join anything, thus labeling themselves a cult—but, if you look closely, you'll find their devil is everyone who hasn't taken the training. There are mass movements without devils, but they seldom attain major status.

In summary, true believers are mentally unbalanced or insecure people, or those without hope or friends. People don't look for allies when they love, but they do when they hate or become obsessed with a cause. And those who desire a new life and a new order feel the old ways must be eliminated before the new order can be built.

Q.

My daughter, who is white and upper middle class, recently joined an organization I consider to be a cult. Upon visiting her, I was surprised to find that those she lived with (over 100) were all white and about the same age. Why?

A.

College sophomores and juniors are considered the ideal cult recruit because they are generally confused and suggestible. They have learned that there is no right or wrong, only shades of grey. Contemporary society has eliminated traditions while thriving on empty consumption, resulting in a mental vacuum. Many students feel a deep need to find something to believe in or belong to.

Cult recruiters will seek out the passively lonely on college campuses. They can usually be found sitting alone, in a cafe or a park. Recruiters avoid the places frequented by the aggressively lonely, such as discos, single's bars and parties. Those most easily seduced are typically from affluent families who haven't positively nurtured their children.

Adept recruiters will go first for those wearing the most

205

expensive clothes. Somatotypes are a factor; mesomorphs and endomorphs are more easily recruited than ectomorphs (the very thin). Insecure body language, such as slumped shoulders, slouched stance or a hanging head, indicates someone seeking acceptance. A shuffling gait may indicate apathy. Face reading is also used to find those most likely to respond.

Cults choose physically attractive, loyal cult members to be recruiters, who then attempt to talk potential members of the opposite sex into attending an introductory meeting or a dinner. Some will even have sex with their target, to draw him or her into the fold. This is the beginning of the conversion process.

HOW TO PRACTICE RADICAL SPIRITUALITY

There are thousands of metaphysical, New Age, and guru-led organizations in the world, and they agree upon very little but *karma* and *reincarnation*. **Radical Spirituality** accepts these concepts and the human-potential logic handed down from Zen to modern-day psychotherapists. You don't need much else to guide you down a powerful path. The rest of the New Age arsenal is smoke and mirrors and complicates your quest.

The following 69 reminders (note the yin/yang symbology and circle of energy in the number) summarize the path. It's the only bible you'll ever need.

1. Your earthly purpose is to integrate your fear-based emotions. Doing so creates an "absence," leaving only your God-self to interact with the world. In your quest to attain the absence, you will sometimes integrate a fear, become fearful again, then integrate the fear again. Don't be discouraged, because one step at a time, you can build a self-actualized foundation that will lead to your goal.

2. Everything you think, say and do creates karma. And that includes the motive, intent and desire behind everything you think, say and do.

3. Karma is the basis of reality, which means you are totally responsible for everything that has ever happened to you.

4. It is your resistance to "what is" (unalterable reality) that causes your suffering.

5. Truth isn't something to be found, it's something you create.

6. Practice meditation, which is training the mind to stay steady on an object without wavering, and cultivating insight to see more clearly the process of things and the nature of dharma.

7. When you don't allow life to fully express itself, you are repressing who you are, and there will be a price to pay.

8. Be patient, compassionate and generous. Accept your kindness as self-serving, and do it anyway.

9. Give up your expectations of others. If they come through, great. If they don't come through, that's okay too.

10. Avoid gurus and religions. They're bad for your mental health and they want your money.

11. Blame is self-pity and incompatible with the acceptance of karma and reincarnation.

12. Incorporate challenge into every aspect of your life to guarantee aliveness. If you don't make your life interesting, your mind will do it for you.

13. Beliefs are not reality, *but* if you want to change your reality, you have to change your beliefs.

14. Don't take things personally. Whoever is giving you grief would be giving grief to anyone who represented to them what you represent.

15. What society calls right and wrong, and moral and immoral is not necessarily so.

16. The point of power is now.

17. Practice being "in the moment."

18. You will always live up to your self-image.

19. You can not become what you resent.

20. Where your attention goes, your energy flows.

21. Wisdom erases karma.

22. When you show mercy, grace and love, you will receive the same in return.

23. You always have free will to choose how you will respond in any situation.

24. When you're upset about the way it is and do nothing to change the situation, you are choosing to allow it to continue.

25. You don't have to be in control to survive.

26. What you leave incomplete, you'll be doomed to repeat.

27. Karma means you don't get away with anything.

28. Within you is everything required to make your life happy and fulfilling.

29. Practice unconditional acceptance of others, by refraining from judgment, blame and expectations.

30. Other people are a mirror for you, because the traits you respond to in others, you recognize in yourself.

31. Everything manifest begins with an idea. Ideas and experiences create beliefs which, in turn, create reality.

32. Awareness is measured by how much you let yourself know of your own truth.

33. Everything you refuse to forgive in yourself and others remains with you as karmic baggage.

34. What other people do does not affect you. What you think about what they do affects you.

35. We are all mirrors of our own thoughts. So unhappiness and failure are self-inflicted while happiness and success are self-bestowed.

36. Every time you get upset with someone else, it is because you have expectations of approval or control (your expectations are in conflict with what is).

37. If you want to understand something or someone, you must observe without criticizing.

38. What you resist you draw to you.

39. Whatever you can conceive and believe, you can achieve, as long as your desires are realistic and do not conflict with the free will of others.

40. What you deny to others will be denied to you.

41. Love others as you would be loved, treasuring their uniqueness while accepting them as they are.

42. The greatest gift you can give another person is to be all of who you are.

43. In your heart you know the right thing to do at each moment in time.

44. You can detach from the chaos in your life by refusing to choose to control the outcome.

45. Your viewpoint determines how you react to life. You're always free to choose a different viewpoint.

46. You need difficult people in your life to provide opportunities to test your resistance to what is.

47. What your mind has created, your mind can change.

48. The primary reason people aren't as happy or fulfilled as they desire to be is that they do not know exactly what they want.

49. Simplicity is one of the key secrets of well-being.

50. Refuse to make a choice based upon the expectations of others. Instead, act in ways consistent with your purpose.

51. Imagination is more powerful than willpower. Change begins with imagination.

52. Practice being centered—physically relaxed, emotionally calm, mentally focused and spiritually aware.

53. Practice persistence. Increasing self-discipline is a matter of building the strength not to give up.

54. Very little in life is really important, so separate what is from what isn't ... and respond only to what is.

55. What you resist you become, if not in this life, in the next (unless you learn to let go of your resistance).

56. In life you experience what you are deeply convinced is so.

57. Value being who you are more than being accepted.

58. You are body/mind/spirit, not body and mind and spirit. What your mind doesn't handle, your body will try to resolve, draining spiritual energy in the process.

59. Suffering is also the source of your awakening.

60. When you're upset or life isn't working, become an "observer" by mentally filtering the situation through the observer's detachment.

61. You will never succeed beyond the size of your vision. So think big.

62. The Universe will support your clearest desires.

63. Pursue your desires with no indecisiveness whatsoever. This assures you of getting what you want.

64. You will achieve self-actualization momentarily, lose it, then go after it again. Eventually it sinks in.

65. Never use fear as a justification for avoiding life.

66. Never do things you will have to karmically punish yourself for.

67. Never do anything that causes you to lose self-esteem.

68. Forgive others, knowing that forgiveness is a selfish act you do for yourself to elevate karma and improve the quality of your life.

69. Wake up.

SELECTED BIBLIOGRAPHY AND RESOURCES

Dick Sutphen Books and Seminars, Box 38, Malibu, CA 90265. Seminars are held annually in various locations on the east and west coast and in Sedona, Arizona. A complete list of metaphysical books are listed on the legal page in the front of this book. Free magazine and catalog.

Dr. Terry Dulin, 735 Old Bethpage Road, Old Bethpage, NY 11804.

Past-Life Therapy: Local recommendations for a therapist : Association for Past-Life Research and Therapies, Inc. Box 20151, Riverside, CA 92516.

Love Without Limits by Deborah Anapol, Ph.D. is available from IntiNet Resource Center, Box 4322, San Rafael, CA 94913. Send $16 plus $3 s&h. Information on IntiNet Resource Center is free with an SASE. Seminars and publications.

For more information on polyfidelity and multimate relationships send an SASE to: Loving More, PEP Publishing, Box 6306, Captain Cook, HI 96704. Seminars and publications.

Myth & Sexuality by Jamake Highwater, New American Library, New York, NY.

Bagwan Shree Rajneesh books: Rebel Publishing House GmbH, Cologne, West Germany & Chidvilas, Box 17550, Boulder, CO 80308.

Many Wonderful Things by Robert W. Huffman and Irene Specht, DeVorss, Marina del Rey, CA.

Everyday Zen by Charlotte Joko Beck, Harper and Row Perennial Library, San Francisco, CA.

Avalanche by W. Brugh Joy, M.D., Ballantine Books, New York, NY.

The Hole In The Ozone Scare by Rogelio Madufo and Ralf Schauerhammer. 21st Century Science Associates, Box 16285, Washington, D.C. 20041.

National Center for Policy Analysis (environmental analysis), 12655 North Central Expressway, Suite 720, Dallas, TX 75243.

Resentment Against Achievement—Understading the Assault Upon Ability by Robert Sheaffer. Prometheus Books, Buffalo, NY.

The True Believer by Eric Hoffer. Perennial Library—Harper & Row, New York, NY.

Battle for the Mind by William Sargent, Pan Books, London.

Waking Up—Overcoming the Obstacles to Human Potential by Charles T. Tart. New Science Library-Shambhala, Boston, MA.

SNAPPING—America's Epidemic of Sudden Personality Change by Flo Conway and Jim Siegelman, Delta Books, Dell Publishing, New York, NY.

Milton Erickson's writings on hypnosis, indirect suggestion, and hypnotic alteration of sensory, perceptual and psychophysiological processes, from various sources.

Ruth Montgomery's books are published by G.P. Putnam's Sons, New York, NY. Paperbacks published by Fawcett, New York, NY.

Edgar Cayce's writings are available through The Association of Research and Enlightenment, Virginia Beach, VA.

In Addition to those already listed, many thanks to all the writers, philosophers and teachers—especially Buddha, Lao Tsu, Dogen, Joshu, Will Schultz, Stewart Emery, Alan Watts, D. T. Suzuki, J. Krishnamurti, Sheldon B. Kopp, Lajos Egri, Robert Anthony, Joe Hyams, Jess Stearn, Brad Steiger, Lauren Meyer, Bruce Lee, Don Weldon, Jimmy Moore, William Glasser, Ed Ford, Shoma Morita, David K. Reynolds, David Richo, Jennifer James, Mihaly Csikszentmihalyi, Taisen Deshimaru, George Leonard, Philip Kapleau, Irmgard Schloegl, Janwillem van de Wetering, Zen Center Los Angeles, and The Center for the Practice of Zen Buddhist Meditation.

About The Author

 Dick Sutphen (pronounced Sut-fen) has written several of the all-time bestselling books on metaphysics and reincarnation, including seven titles for Simon and Schuster Pocket Books, who call him "America's foremost psychic researcher." *You Were Born Again To Be Together* has sold nearly a million copies. Other recent titles include: *Finding Your Answers Within, Earthly Purpose, The Oracle Within, Reinventing Yourself* and *The Spiritual Path Guidebook. Heart Magic* is a collection of Dick's mystical fiction about finding love and answers.

Over 100,000 people have attended a Sutphen Seminar, which are conducted every year in major cities. "The 5-Day Professional Past-Life-Therapy Training" is conducted in the Los Angeles area and teaches people to hypnotize and regress others. Dick has also created over 200 audio and video mind-programming tapes and CDs now in world-wide release. He lives with his wife Tara and their children in Malibu, California.

Writing Dick Sutphen: Requests to be added to the magazine mailing list, and letters about personal metaphysical experiences are always welcome. But due to the volume of mail, Dick can not answer personally, other than in his "Controversial Questions" column.

FREE MAGAZINE

Dick and Tara Sutphen publish a quarterly magazine that is mailed to 200,000 book/tape buyers and seminar attendees. A sample issue is free, and if you purchase or attend a seminar, the publication is mailed free for two years. If you purchased this book in a bookstore, send the receipt (or a copy) and we'll add you to the mailing list for two years.

Each issue is approximately 80 pages and contains news, research reports and articles on metaphysics, psychic exploration and self-help, in addition to providing information on Sutphen Seminars, and 300 audio and video tapes: hypnosis, meditation, sleep programming, subliminal programming, silent subliminals and inner-harmony music.

Books From Valley of the Sun

☐ **How To Absolutely, Positively Look 5 to 10 Years Younger**
By Sharon Boyd . . . . . . B937—$12.00

☐ **How To Believe In Nothing & Set Yourself Free**
By Michael Misita . . . . . . B936—$9.98

☐ **50 Spiritually Powerful Meditations**
By Margaret Rogers . . . . B934—$9.98

☐ **The Soulmate Process**
By Bob Lancer . . . . B928—$9.98

☐ **The Spiritual Path Guidebook**
By Dick Sutphen . . . . . . B930—$5.95

☐ **Reinventing Yourself**
By Dick Sutphen . . . . . . B927—$9.98

☐ **Blame It On Your Past Lives**
By Tara Sutphen . . . . . . B933—$9.98

☐ **Yoga, Youth & Reincarnation**
By Jess Stearn . . . . B935—$9.98

☐ **Sedona: Psychic Energy Vortexes**
. . . . B922—$9.98

☐ **Heart Magic**
By Dick Sutphen . . . . . . B926—$9.98

☐ **The Nasty Dragon Who Became A Nice Puppy**
By Dick Sutphen . . . . . . B929—$10.98

☐ **Past-Life Therapy In Action**
By Dick Sutphen & Lauren L. Taylor
. . . . B915—$7.95

☐ **Enlightenment Transcripts**
By Dick Sutphen . . . . . . B923—$3.95

☐ **The Star Rover**
By Jack London . . . . B914—$8.95

☐ **Assertiveness Training**
By Dick Sutphen . . . . . . B980—$3.95

☐ **A Veil Too Thin**
By Betty Riley . . . . B920—$2.95

☐ **Tape Instruction & Idea Manual**
. . . . B912—$2.95

From Simon & Schuster Pocket Books

☐ **You Were Born Again To Be Together**
By Dick Sutphen . . . . . . B904—$5.99

☐ **Past Lives, Future Loves**
By Dick Sutphen . . . . . . B905—$4.95

☐ **The Oracle Within**
By Dick Sutphen . . . . . . B909—$9.95

☐ **Earthly Purpose**
By Dick Sutphen . . . . . . B908—$4.95

☐ **Finding Your Answers Within**
By Dick Sutphen . . . . . . B907—$4.50

Audio/Video Tapes That Relate To This Book
Available Through Your Local Metaphysical Bookseller Or Directly From Valley of the Sun Publishing

RX17® Audio Programming

Side A: Hypnosis. **Side B:** Subliminal suggestions hidden in soothing music. One hour. Boxed in slip case.

Past-Life Regression
RX201—$12.50

Concentration Power Plus
RX126—$12.50

2-Tape Albums

Contains 2 audio cassette tapes & Instruction Manual.

Past-Life Therapy
AX901—$24.95

Assertiveness Training
C802—$24.95

Video Hypnosis®

4 kinds of mind programming, including subliminal audio and video. Thirty minutes, VHS only.

Master of Life
VHS105—$19.95

Past-Life Regression
VHS129—$19.95

Self-Discipline
VHS147—$19.95

Zen Attitude
VHS151—$19.95

Incredible Concentration
VHS116—$19.95

4-Tape Hypnosis Album

Four hypnosis tapes (8 sessions) & instruction book in a vinyl album.

Past-Life Hypnotic Regression Course
Volume I . . . . C801—$39.95

CD Meditation Journeys

A unique new kind of meditation journey with 3-D sound. The story processes you as you explore. Over an hour, on CD.

Temple of Light . . . . . CD777—$14.95

Gateless Gate . . . . CD778—$14.95

Audio Workshop

Contains all the training you need to become a good hypnosis subject.

How To Be A Better Receiver In Hypnosis
NX502—$12.50

These titles may be purchased at your local New Age store, or you may order them direct from **Valley of the Sun Publishing**. VISA, MasterCard and American Express orders, call toll-free: 1-800-421-6603, or make checks payable to **Valley of the Sun Publishing**. Mail to: **Valley of the Sun,** Box 38, Malibu, CA 90265